Heart Ink

Jason Moppin

Heart Ink

Get Inked God's Way

A note from Pastor Jason Moppin

I wrote this book burdened for God's people to get a better sense for how much God loves them and desires a close, intimate relationship with them.

It is an attempt to get people to recognize that still small voice within, to hear and respond to God when He speaks. And to let His words be written on your hearts and allow them to eternally change you forever.

Heart Ink is a book that I believe God asked me to write. I just hope and pray that I wrote down the things that He wanted me to, and that it ministers to whoever reads it.

Heart Ink

Jason Moppin

© 2020 Emmanuel Books, LLC.

All rights reserved. No part of this publication may be reproduced, stored in a retrieval system or transmitted in any form or by any means, electronic, mechanical, photocopying, recording or otherwise without the prior permission of the publisher or in accordance with the provisions of the Copyright, Designs and Patents Act 1988 or under the terms of any license permitting limited copying issued by the Copyright Licensing Agency.

Published by:
Emmanuel Books, LLC.
34509 Globe School Ave.
Edwards, MO, USA

Typesetting: Times New Roman

Cover Design: Emmanuel Books, LLC

Unless otherwise noted, scripture quotations are taken from the HOLY BIBLE: NEW ENGLISH STANDARD VERSION ®. The English Standard Version is a trademark registered in the United States Patent and Trademark Office.

ISBN-978-1-7331211-3-2 (HC)

ISBN-978-1-7331211-4-9 (PB)

ISBN - 978-1-7331211-6-3 (Ebook)

Printed in the United States of America

Hello, to whoever finds themselves reading a copy of this book, Heart Ink.

I am writing this book to address not a new problem, but a large epidemic in our world today that is affecting even those that are a part of the church. Grace and peace be to you from our heavenly Father and our Lord Jesus Christ. I pray that your heart be open and receptive to what you read, and that God opens the eyes of your understanding; that you find a new hunger and thirst for God and His word like never before. I pray that you are eternally changed by what you read in this book and allow God to write on your heart every time you read His word. Amen.

Forward

When Jason invited me to write a foreword for his "Heart Ink" book, I was honored to accept. I was honored because of the relationship that Jason and I have had through the years! I was privileged to be his Pastor and watch him grow in the Lord! Jason has a Pastor's heart and a great love for God's word! This is a must read book for all Christians to see how God moves personally.

It has been a pleasure for me to read the manuscript, and I feel that I should encourage every potential reader to enjoy these pages as I have done. Jason gives a heartfelt approach that all can relate to with his testimony and life experiences. This is a book that shows how active the Triune God works to perform His good and perfect will!
Bro. Paul Stephens

CHAPTER I

The Epidemic and Hearing God's Voice

Many of us know sheep are the kind of animal in need of a shepherd, someone to care for them, someone to protect them from the enemy, someone to call them back to the herd. Often times, people are referred to as sheep in scripture such as when Jesus said in John 10: 27:

"My *sheep hear My voice and follow Me.*"

Oftentimes when we find ourselves telling someone today that God spoke to us or told us something, unfortunately, we get that crazy look from them. The truth is that God speaks to a lot more people than one would actually think. The problem is, when we tend to think it was us, in and of ourselves that we had a particularly good idea or thought, when in reality, it came from God. When the Holy Spirit is not given credit for such occasions is when it all becomes rather unfortunate.

According to James 1:17:

"Every good and perfect gift comes from God."

Since The Bible says this, it must also be true with our thoughts.

Phil 4:8 tells us that

"Whatever is true, noble, right, pure, lovely, admirable, excellent, praiseworthy; to think on these things because they are from God."

All these good thoughts and ideas, being kind and generous to someone; those are fruits of the Holy Spirit.

Galatians 5:22-23 *"But the fruit of the spirit is love, joy, peace, patience, kindness, goodness, gentleness, faithfulness, and self-control. Against such things there is no law.*

If we would pay more attention to the fact it all comes from Him and give Him the credit, we would be more sensitive and tuned into what His voice sounds like when we hear it during other times.

Proverbs 29:18 says, *"Where there is no prophetic vision the people cast off restraint, but blessed is he who keeps the law."*

Hosea 4:6 says, *"My people are destroyed for lack of knowledge; because you have rejected knowledge, I reject you from being a priest to me. And since you have forgotten the law of your God, I also will forget your children."*

We don't expect the world to know what God's voice sounds like or even know much about Him, but the church should. His sheep, the people of His pasture, should know His mighty voice.

CHAPTER 2

Coming Back Home

I was raised in church and saved at an early age, but didn't live for God like I should have. I just didn't think I could live for God without any of my close friends being saved along with me. I prayed for them earnestly, but when it didn't seem like salvation was going to happen for them, I told God I couldn't do it either. I was sorry, but I just couldn't live for Him, not now. I consciously walked away from the Lord. Some may say I never was really saved then, but only God knows. I know what I experienced. I felt the difference after having confessed with my mouth and believed in my heart that Jesus was Lord like the Bible says to do, but like the Prodigal Son, I wanted what was mine, I was leaving, and I did.

I lived like the devil for the next three or four years or so. I was backslidden and lost, I didn't even try to live for God. I seemed to be more aware of spiritual things than others my own age, but never really let God get a hold of my life until the summer before my senior year of high school. I went to church camp that summer under protest. My mom wanted me to go, but I didn't want to. I thank God for all the praying moms out there that can see things in the spiritual realm others can't. It was like she knew it was now or never for me. There was an urgency that she had for me to go that I will never forget.

Reluctantly, I went to camp, but I was spiritually dead. I was sixteen and backslidden as I could be, completely out of relationship with God. I remember in one of the evening services that our pastor's oldest son, about nineteen at that time, came over to me where I was sitting and asked me to go forward and pray with his younger brother.

He was at the altar with a group of other teens crying out to God for various reasons. I decided to go forward to play along and get him off my back, so I acted like I was praying for a while then stepped back. I thought I would stand around for a few more minutes then go back to my seat. Just before I left the altar, I saw a kid I recognized walking in my direction. God completely changed his life a couple years earlier. God had saved him and called him to preach; the transformation that had taken place in this kid's life was miraculous. He was heading straight for me.

He asked if everything was okay, to which I replied, "Yes," but he said, "No, I mean if you died tonight, where would your soul spend eternity?" I told him Hell. He asked me if I wanted to go to Heaven, to which I responded, "Well yea, doesn't everybody?" He asked if he could pray with me, and I told him that I had been raised in church and was aware of how this all worked. I knew I couldn't be saved unless the Holy Spirit was convicting me or drawing me in. Honestly, I hadn't felt any conviction or Him drawing me in for quite some time. He asked if he could just pray that the Holy Spirit would deal with me and I agreed.

    He grabbed a young pastor that was standing close by and explained to him what I had said. He told him how the Holy Spirit hadn't dealt with me in a long time and I had agreed to let them pray that He would. I figured they would just pray a bit and move on, but these men started praying fervently and passionately over me; they were Holy Ghost filled prayers in English that I could understand, and the Spirit of God came over me like a blanket. The conviction and pull of the Holy Spirit were so strong. I repented and asked God to save me and come back into my life again, and He did. I remember crying out to God and asking Him to take me back and if He would, I would never drift that far away from Him again, and I never have. That was an awesome time at the altar praying for forgiveness and thanking God for it. It was unmistakable what He had done for me that night.

CHAPTER 3

Strength and Determination

The next couple of nights at the altar, I spent all my time and efforts praying again for all my friends to get saved. To be fair, I told God He could have the rest of the summer until school started to accomplish this.

You see, I still didn't think I could live for Him all by myself. In one of these altar services, God spoke to me through a mentor/pastor friend I really looked up to then and still do. He came over and knelt down with me while I was praying. I was not praying out loud at all and there was no way he could have known what I was praying for without God revealing it to him. Well, God must have been revealing it, because he came over to me and said God told him to come tell me that I needed to stop praying for everyone I knew and pray for strength and determination so I could live for Him. I did. The rest of my time at church camp, that is what I prayed for, and I allowed God to write that upon my heart. It has eternally changed me - that was in June and July of 1992, and God has been writing things upon my heart ever since.

CHAPTER 4

God's Call

God called me to preach that same year. I was just sixteen years old turning seventeen, and scared to death not knowing why God would call me into the ministry or how He was going to accomplish it, but He did. This was going to require me listening and being willing to do what He asked and allowing Him to continue to write on my heart.

After just a few months while attending church, it seemed like every time I prayed, God would begin dealing with me about preaching His word. Every time I got down to pray, all I would hear Him say was, "I want you to preach My word." This went on for a few weeks and I kept telling God no. I told Him, He didn't really want me to preach because there was no way I could do it; my dad wasn't a preacher and I didn't come from any line of preachers.

During this time in my life, I believed preachers came from preachers, for whatever reason, that's just what it seemed like to me. It was just that this was the case for most of the ministers I knew at that time. God wasn't taking no for an answer, and He didn't let up on me until I made a pact with Him either. Now I don't recommend fleecing God nor will He always allow it, but if He does you can bet He will hold up His end of the bargain. We can learn this from Judges 6:36-40 as it says,

"Then Gideon said to God, "If you will save Israel by my hand, as you have said, behold, I am laying a fleece of wool on the threshing floor. If there is dew on the fleece alone, and it is dry on all the ground, then I shall know that you will save Israel by my hand, as you have said." "And it was so. When he rose early the next morning and squeezed the fleece, he wrung enough dew from the fleece to fill a bowl with water. Then Gideon said to God, "let not your anger burn against me; let me speak just once more. Please let me test just once more with the fleece. Please let it be dry on the fleece only, and on all the ground let there be dew." And God did so that night; and it was dry on the fleece only, and on all the ground there was dew."

CHAPTER 5

Seeking the Baptism

I was raised in an old school Pentecostal church that believed in and operated in the gifts of the Spirit. I didn't know any preachers that weren't gifted with that of speaking in other tongues like in Acts.

Acts 2:4 *"And they were filled with the Holy Spirit and began to speak in other tongues as the Spirit gave them utterance."*

You see, I hadn't received this particular gift yet.

1 Corinthians 12:4-11

"Now concerning spiritual gifts, brothers, I do not want you to be uninformed. You know that when you were pagans you were led astray to mute idols, however you were led. Therefore I want you to understand that no one speaking in the Spirit of God ever says, 'Jesus is accursed!' and no one can say, 'Jesus is Lord' except in the Holy Spirit. Now there are varieties of gifts, but the same Spirit; and

there are varieties of service, but the same Lord; and there are varieties of activities, but it is the same God who empowers them all in everyone. To each is given the manifestation of the Spirit for the common good. For to one is given through the Spirit the utterance of wisdom, and to another the utterance of knowledge according to the same Spirit, to another faith by the same Spirit, to another gifts of healing by the one Spirit, to another the working of miracles, to another prophecy, to another the ability to distinguish between spirits, to another various kinds of tongues, to another the interpretation of tongues. All these are empowered by one and the same spirit, who apportions to each one individually as he wills."

The point was that I did not have the gift of speaking in other tongues yet, which was very important in the Pentecostal church I attended, and I wasn't going to tell anyone that God was calling me to preach. The deal was that if He would fill me with the Holy Spirit, with the evidence of speaking in other tongues, I would accept His call and step out and tell everyone what God was calling me to do. My end of the bargain was that I would seek earnestly for it. You see, I hadn't done that yet because I had been focusing on praying for strength and determination to live for Him. Sometimes we have not because we ask not.

According to Matthew 7: 7, 8:

"Ask and you shall receive, seek and you shall find, knock and it will be opened unto you."

I told the Lord I would seek earnestly and do anything asked of me in the church no matter what it was, and I did. I spoke at youth groups, I taught Sunday school if needed, I prayed over offerings, took up testimonies and closed in prayer, anything to help prepare me for what God was calling me to do.

For about two years, I sought the Lord for the baptism of the Holy Spirit. I extended church services for long periods of time praying so intently for this particular gift, that I remember when I looked up after finishing praying, the only ones left were the musicians, the pastor and his family, and mine. Everyone else had already left. I don't want to make it sound like it should be hard to receive this particular gift The Bible speaks about, because it should not be hard to receive. However, we sometimes make things more difficult than they should. God wants us to have all of His gifts.

1 Corinthians 14:5 *"Now I want you all to speak in tongues, but even more to prophesy. The one who prophesies is greater than the one who speaks in tongues, unless someone interprets, so that the church may be built up."*

Acts 2:38-39 says, *"Repent and be baptized every one of you in the name of Jesus Christ for the forgiveness of your sins, and you will receive the gift of the Holy Spirit. For the promise is for you and for your children and for all who are far off, everyone whom the Lord our God calls to himself."*

I believe sometimes my fellow Pentecostal believers do not seek the baptism because they know they do not need it to go to Heaven. Therefore they wonder, why seek it? While it is true that we do not necessarily need the gift of the baptism in the Holy Spirit to go to Heaven, I do not believe God would offer this gift to us if He did not wish we had it. It was given to us so we could live bold and empowered lives. God would not offer this gift to us, and wish that all men had it, and want His Son to baptize us in it if there were no benefit for us in receiving it.

    I believe it is the lack of understanding for those believers who are seeking the baptism of the Holy Spirit that makes it difficult to receive. I do not know of any one person who would leave a Christmas present with his or her name on it under the tree unopened. We open all our presents with anticipation and excitement. However, when it comes to God's gifts that He leaves for us with our names on them, paid for by the blood of His own Son, sometimes those are left unopened or even undesired. To those who are seeking the gifts, do not be discouraged and do not make it too hard. It is critical to get yourself out of the way and just receive. Reference 1 Corinthians 12:4-11 during this time.

From my own experience, I know I was making it too difficult. I was confused about what to expect when it would actually happen to me. This was probably because of all of the different stories I heard growing up in the Pentecostal church about how and when it happened to those who had already received the baptism. Sometimes it was described as being some kind of out of body experience. Perhaps that was how it happened to them, but that just simply was not the case for me, nor most people I have talked with about this.

It was late winter after I graduated that I moved to Shawnee Mission, Kansas, because of a job offer. I lived there with my great aunt and uncle who pastored a big church in that area. These two people were two of the godliest individuals that I had ever known and were modern day patriarchs and matriarchs of our family. There was a large youth group that was on fire for God within the church. Living in the Kansas City area allowed me the opportunity to go to different youth groups at different churches almost every night of the week if I wanted, and that's what I did most of the time.

One of the youth groups I attended often was having a tent revival on a new piece of property that the church had recently purchased so they could build to fit the growing church. I attended the tent revival in Liberty, Missouri, after not having sought for the baptism in a while, and that is exactly what the preacher was preaching on. I was so convicted that when he was barely done preaching, I ran down to the front to pray. Bales of hay in front of a flatbed trailer served as the altar. I stood there; hands raised, and crying out to God to fill me with the Holy Spirit. God truly did something for me that night. Most likely, He gifted me because I let Him lead. Instead of focusing on how I thought things would take place when He would fill me with the Holy Spirit, I just let Him lead.

No sooner than I got to the front and started praying, I got a knot in my stomach. It was a horrible cramping pain. For a minute, I thought I might even throw up. I looked for a place to kneel down because I thought maybe if I bent over it would help with the pain, but I said to myself, "No, I'm praying through this and I'm receiving the baptism tonight." I asked God to take the pain away, but it just intensified. I pressed through the pain and prayed for the baptism in the Holy Spirit. The same prayer language that would always come to me every time before when I would seek the baptism came back. I would never let it out though because I thought it was just me making something up.

I thought it sounded too much like other people's prayer languages, so I would never just speak it and let it out. I was always too aware of what was going on around me. It was never some hypnotic out of body experience that I had heard about, especially this time. I seriously thought I was going to vomit in front of everyone, but this time it didn't bother me much because I didn't know very many people who were there, so I just let it all out. I was completely aware of my surroundings and what was happening; I consciously started to pray out loud in the same prayer language that would always come to me. Immediately, I mean instantly, the cramp in my stomach was gone the moment that I started praying in my prayer language. It was so noticeable that I thought, "Wow, the pain's gone."

Then God spoke John 7:38,39 to me. He said, *"Out of your belly shall flow rivers of living water. This He spoke about the Holy Spirit that was not yet given."*

God confirmed what He did for me that night with His Word. It was the same prayer language that wanted to come out all along. I was waiting for something to happen from the outside in but when it happened, it was from the inside out.

    The Holy Spirit already lives in us upon salvation, but he wants to flow out of us a perpetually, never stopping, ever flowing stream of living water.

CHAPTER 6

Feed My Sheep

I prayed for a while and went back to my seat feeling overwhelmed with joy that I had finally received what I had been praying for and what God was longing to give me. Not long after I got back to my seat, conviction came over me like I had never before felt. I did not understand what was happening. It seemed like I went from the mountaintop to the valley in just seconds. I started weeping all over again and telling God that I loved Him. I remember telling God over and over that I loved Him. I remember saying, "God, You know I love You!"

Similarly, John says in John 21:15-*17*

"When they had finished breakfast, Jesus said to Simon Peter, 'Simon, son of John, do you love me more than these?' He said to him, 'Yes, Lord; you know that I love you.' He said to him, 'Feed my lambs.' He said to him a second time, 'Simon, son of John, do you love me?' He said to him, 'Yes, Lord; you know that I love you.' He said to him, 'Tend my sheep.' He said to him a third time, 'Simon,

son of John, do you love me?' Peter was grieved because he said to him the third time, 'Do you love me?' and he said to him, 'Lord, you know everything; you know that I love you.' Jesus said to him, 'Feed my sheep.'"

Then God asked me if I remembered our "deal". I knew I was being held accountable.

I thought, "Oh man!"

I had forgotten about it. Now all the fear and anxiety were flooding back in. It wasn't until I said,

"Okay, God, I will preach Your word", that fear left.

Of course, I still get nervous about speaking at different occasions, but the crippling fear of simply telling people what God was calling me to do left when I said, "Okay Lord, I'll do it."

A few weeks passed, and I was trying to awake to get ready for work early one morning when God plainly spoke to me. He said, "How can you fulfill the call I have on your life with the job you have now?" That woke me up in a hurry and I thought about it and said, "You're right Lord, I can't." I put my notice in at work, worked my two weeks, and moved back home to a slower paced life, so I could focus on His call that He had on my life.

CHAPTER 7

We Serve God Not Man

God started dealing with me about going to a different church. Oftentimes, within my church, it was frowned upon to hop from one church to another; they called it church hopping and no one wanted to be branded a church hopper. I was very distraught and prayed very hard for clarity, but God wasn't letting up, and I knew what He wanted me to do.

I remember one night at church this dear elderly lady came over to pray with me; she was a retired minister's wife and a dear saint of God. She could tell I was carrying a heavy burden for something and wanted to help if she could. She asked if she could help me pray for something. I told her I would rather not say, but that Yes, I needed prayer. She asked a few more questions wanting more information on what was going on – thinking the world of her and her husband I told her that I felt like God was dealing with me about going to a different church.

"OH NO!" she said. She told me to please not make any rash decisions, and to be sure it was God. But she didn't believe God would be telling me to do that.

No sooner than the words came out of her mouth, God spoke so clear to me to listen to Him not her. Then He said, "You serve Me not man."

Luke 4:8, *"You shall worship the Lord your God, and him only shall you serve."*

I simply bowed my head and continued to pray. It was less than a minute when she turned around in the pew and told me to forget what she had just said because God had just told her to tell me, "I serve Him and not man." WOW! I told her God had just spoken that to me as she was talking to me the first time. She told me God had just confirmed His word and she knew it was not going to be an easy thing telling my mom, granny, and my pastor that I was leaving, but it was something I was going to have to do because God instructed it.

It was hard and not everyone understood as change is extremely difficult. I'm sure some thought I was not hearing from God, but I am glad I learned at an early age that we serve God and not man. It's a lesson we must all learn if we are going to try to follow Him closely. I would soon learn God would remind me of this again.

CHAPTER 8

Another Move

The church I was led to was incredible. The pastor and his wife took me in, they loved me; they allowed me to preach often. For that I will ever be thankful. After about a year, God asked me to leave. I thought, surely not, I could not do this again. I bargained, begged, and tried to do anything to keep from leaving, but the conviction and clarity of what to do was so strong. I stayed for a while longer not wanting to leave. Then one Sunday morning, a lady, not knowing my story or even that God was dealing with me about leaving, gave a message in tongues. It was then interpreted and the message was: "I have told you what to do but you have hardened your heart and stiffened your neck against Me. It's time for you to repent and remember that you serve Me, not man!"

Needless to say, I hit the altar and repented and prayed for strength to step out and do what God wanted me to do. I told the pastor that morning that I would not be back that night for the evening service. I would have to catch up with him later in the week to talk. I was too emotional to talk about it then. I really didn't understand what God was doing, but that's one of the greatest things about The Lord God Almighty; we don't have to understand, we just have to follow and listen.

God proved sovereign yet again as the church to which I was lead just so happened to be where I met my wife. God had great plans for me as He would soon lead me to an entire group of people that are still in my life today.

I was able to sit under an outstanding preacher/teacher of God's Word, a man that God has used mightily in my life and still does to this day. He has been someone to encourage and push me to be more than I am, and teach me to continually grow in the Lord. God used him greatly to help me get past a lot of dogmatic mindsets of legalism that I was raised around, and let God speak more clearly through His scripture. He was the first and maybe the only one who told me that he didn't understand why I was the only one who couldn't see my own potential. I'm sure that's the case in a lot of our lives. For about four or five years or so, I gleaned all I could from him. The church and people were amazing, and God used them to eternally change my life.

CHAPTER 9

Preparation

During a revival in 1999, in one of the altar services, God spoke something to me. He said He was going to prepare me to be with my people, but I didn't understand what He meant completely. The only thing I thought I knew was that He must have meant my hometown. The church I was attending was a couple of towns over, about 30 minutes away. Again, all I was sure about was that God meant Climax Springs, MO.

After about a year, a man called from a little church in Climax Springs and asked if I would come preach for them and to pray about pastoring the church. It was not the same church I grew up in but a different little Pentecostal church. You see, the retired minister whose wife confirmed God's Word that I serve Him and not man - they had been filling in for a while along with another retired minister, who now have both gone on to be with the Lord. They told the leaders of the little church to call me and see if I would come and preach for them. I told them I would preach for two Sundays, and then I would like some time to pray about it. Deep down in my heart of hearts, I already knew what I should do.

After I preached there for a couple of Sundays, I went back to the church I was attending and went in early to pray one Sunday night before service. I really asked God to speak crystal clear to me because my decision didn't just affect me now, but my wife and both of our families. The pastor knew what I was praying about and he was praying for me as well.

This particular Sunday night, I remember hearing him come into the church as I was praying, and he went to his office. When I was done, I got up and went back into his office. He asked if I had made my decision yet and I let him know I had not yet. He began to tell me that he had been thinking of talking to the people of the church about putting me on staff as an assistant pastor or something similar. The church was running about 250 attendees on Sunday mornings, and he thought it could support an assistant pastor. He did not know my story or that I had just prayed for God to speak crystal clear to me so I could know for sure what to do. He said, "But that's just my plan of what I was thinking, you must do what God is telling you to do because you serve God and not man."

I started crying when he spoke those words to me and he asked what it was he said. I told him the story and he said, "Okay, that is crazy!" Our church understood and blessed us with a huge love offering and bought Bible commentaries for us when we left. Many of the dear people are still a huge part of my life today.

CHAPTER 10

God Speaks in Dark Times

"Joy is a Choice"

I don't want anyone to get the wrong impression that all I have are mountain top experiences of God revealing things to me. I've had my share of low times too. Depression has been something that I've had my battles with, to the point of being suicidal many times in my younger years and young adult life. Probably my darkest time was shortly after my wife, Melissa, and I got married. It was hard.

We were two young strong-willed people learning how to live together and get through a lot of struggles financially, mentally, and spiritually. I'm thankful that no matter how dark it became, and no matter how far I drifted away, God still desired to speak to me, and He did. Sometimes He speaks the clearest in those moments.

I remember leaving the house one day ready to end it all because of all my overwhelming problems. I just couldn't see how God could fix them. He said to me, "It's sad that for several years you have been telling people to hang in there because God was bigger than their problems, but you can't believe that I am bigger than yours."

It was really convicting and stopped me from doing anything that day, but I still wasn't delivered from the darkness of depression and the load of cares and condemnation I was carrying around.

Shortly afterward, I was still battling with the desire not to live and go on. I still remember the stretch of road I was on, wanting to drive my car off of the road into a big tree and end it all when God spoke to me and said, *"This only bothers you because you let it!"* and then He said, *"Joy is really a choice, you have to choose it!"*

I thought, *"That's it?" "It's not worked for, or obtained by laboring, it's a choice?" "It's received?" "It's a gift?"* Then I knew, yes, it is! Now I'm sure there are many more educated individuals out there that have known this for a long time. I'm sure there are even entire books written about it, but until God wrote it on my own heart, I did not fully understand. Until The Lord God Almighty Himself writes it on your own heart and makes it a revelation to you, it may not help. I'm here today to tell anyone reading this, that if you will choose joy today over your problems and allow God to write that on your heart, the darkness of depression will start to disappear out of your life.

When I chose to not let those things bother me like they were, and not to let them rob my peace and joy and started speaking joy and peace over my life - things changed for me. I'm not telling you that things don't ever bother me and that I don't have bad days, but the oppressive darkness that kept me captive is gone, and it has never had a hold of me like that since. I'm sure glad that God knows what He is doing. I can promise you, I've been through worse and more depressing things since then, but I'm not that same person I was then. I've got a lot more Heart Ink and that makes a big difference in how things affect me. You can still pray for me though, I need it, and I will pray that the word of God will change your life as well, and that God comes more alive to you than ever before.

CHAPTER 11

Chasing Fellowship

It was the spring of 2001 when I took my first senior pastoring position at the small church in my small hometown that had previously called. When I say small, my wife and I made for a total of eight in the church, and the town had less than one hundred people in the city limits - it is small. I was about twenty-four years old, green as grass, just a pup, still wet behind the ears. I never went to seminary or college, and I barely graduated high school. Before then, I preached every chance I got, read my Bible, taught Sunday school, and worked with youth. I did everything I could to learn all I could because I knew what God had called me to do. I was a little overwhelmed and under confident in myself and I found myself thinking I needed that peer group again.

    The Ministerial Alliance in our town had some good pastors. Some had agreed to meet for Bible studies monthly which I greatly needed as well as fellowship with other ministers. When most of those who had a stronger desire to fellowship together moved on, and out of our community, it left me burdened down still desiring that fellowship. I felt like it didn't seem to be nearly as important to the ministers that were still left in our community then. I felt like there was a spirit of competition among them that was disheartening. I tried many things to pull the group together, mainly because I felt as though I had to have it. I did this for several years until I was just completely worn out of chasing fellowship with ministers inside and outside of our little town.

One day, I just threw my hands up and told God I couldn't do it anymore. If these guys didn't feel the need to help a young brother or get along and have good fellowship together, then I guess I didn't need them. I wasn't writing anyone off, and I'm not saying we don't need each other, because we do. I just stopped looking to them to fill a role in my life that God wanted to fill. I remember crying out to God and saying, "Well God, I guess it's just You and me." I realize it wasn't, but that's how it felt. I think that's what God was waiting for. He was waiting for me to realize that He is enough and that His Grace is Sufficient.

Jesus even said so in: 2 Corinthians 12:9, *"My grace is sufficient for you, for my power is made perfect in weakness."*

I've learned I am more successful, confident, and strong when I am not depending on man, but God, allowing Him to perfect His power in me though my weaknesses.

CHAPTER 12

The Great Teacher

I have had the privilege of sitting under some very good pastors and teachers in my young Christian life, some men and women of God that I have learned a lot from, but I've never had anyone teach me like the Holy Spirit.

John 14:26 says, *"But the Helper, the Holy Spirit, whom the Father will send in my name, he will teach you all things and bring to your remembrance all that I have said to you."*

This is what He was sent here to do. I thank God for the good Bible teaching I've had, but I should not look to man to fulfill the Holy Spirit's role in my life. I've learned we need to give Him the chance to be our number one teacher. I've learned more in daily Bible study than anywhere else, and I know God will do the same for all of us. Don't believe man because he said something; believe God because He wrote it on your heart. It is not our pastor's job to be the sole source of our spiritual growth. I hope God is using your pastor mightily in all of our lives. We should be growing and learning in church, but man will fall short of what we need at times. God will not.

CHAPTER 13

Seek God First

I know the Bible teaches us to seek Godly counsel, but there is no Godlier council than from God Himself. He is the Spirit of counsel and might! God is the One that truly knows all things and knows how to solve every problem. Go to Him first and give Him a chance to do what His word says He will do.

There was a time in my life where I was searching for answers to things that I was not so sure how to hear God. Typically, I would go to a dear friend or pastor of mine to seek advice and wisdom, but this was a different story. I had a situation arise, so I went to him and asked what I should do because I didn't know and didn't think I could hear the voice of God clear enough to get His Will. I told him I would do whatever he said, that's how much this individual meant to me.

The problem was that I hadn't sought God first for the answer myself. I was actually driving home from our visit when God told me what to do. By now, you can guess it wasn't what my pastor friend had advised, so I had to tell him that I was going to go a different route. He wondered why because I told him I trusted him and would do whatever he thought I should do. It's very difficult when one needs to take back things said and promises made, but when God intervenes and asks us to do something; we need to do it because He knows best. Fortunately, this individual understood and wished me the best, but it could have all been avoided had I given God the chance to speak first. This was not to say I got bad advice, it's just that God knows all things and can do all things, He can even speak clearly enough to be heard in chaotic circumstances if we just be still and listen to the still small voice of God.

CHAPTER 14

New Vision

God was still speaking to me and writing things on my heart up to that time, but I can say things seemed to explode for me spiritually when I quit chasing fellowship with men. I do believe we need good fellowship with man, but we are to chase God and not man. When I was okay with it just being God and me, and I looked to Him to fill all those roles in my life, He did. I had a new vision, a revelation of scripture, and understanding. It was the biggest turning point in my walk with Christ to date for sure. We need more of Him, not people. Please do not misunderstand, people are not bad. I still have great pastor friends and mentors I call when I need to talk. I thank God for the ones that are there for me, but I cannot look to them to fill God's role in my life.

The Bible says in 2 Corinthians 3:3, *"And you show that you are a letter from Christ delivered by us, written not with ink but with the Spirit of the living God, not on tablets of stone but on tablets of human hearts."*

I found it truly incredible to know that a letter from Christ, God writes on our hearts by His Spirit, and our lives are an open epistle for all to read. I pray we are positive so others can read clearly what it says with no mixed messages about God. I pray it might not be confusing nor turn others away from Christ. Let's let mankind read how a Holy loving God wants a relationship with His creation made in His likeness, how He wants all people to come to the saving knowledge of Jesus Christ.

CHAPTER 15

Heart Ink

Figuratively speaking, God needs to be our tattoo artist. It's His longing to write these things on our hearts that will change us forever.

Jeremiah 31:33 says, *"This is the covenant I will make with the house of Israel after that time, declares the Lord. I will put My law in their minds and write it on their hearts. I will be their God and they will be My people."*

God can do more in our lives in just moments than man can do in years. A few years back, God started dealing with me about writing a book. God gave me the title to this book because of the time and culture in which we live. Everybody wants to get inked. Tattoos seem to be the preferred method of which to remember and memorialize things. When asked, most people never forget why they got their tattoos or where they were when they got them.

Similarly, when we allow God to start writing on our hearts, we will not forget. I hope to continue to let Him write my story and I pray He will continue to write your story.

Hebrews 12:2 says, "Looking to Jesus, the founder (author) and perfecter (finisher) of our faith, who for the joy that was set before him endured the cross, despising the shame, and is seated at the right hand of the throne of God."

I struggled for a few years about writing this book, again because of insecurities. I felt like such a hypocrite, having never read a book other than the Bible and commentaries. See Spot Run or Green Eggs and Ham might have been on my reading list, but seriously, how could I expect anyone to buy or read this book laid upon my heart when I've never read one for myself? I don't read well, and I have reading comprehension problems.

It takes me hours to read and understand what most do in minutes. I have to read and re-read over and over to actually understand something. For the limited time I have with family, work, life, church - when I spend time reading something it is going to be scripture or commentary on scripture. If I have any good quiet time, I would feel bad reading anything else, not that you should, I just do.

It is so crucial that we, as God's people, start allowing Him to reveal His word to us and write it on our hearts. If not, they are just words on a page. Until the revelations of the prophets and apostles become ours too, they won't make the everlasting difference they were meant to make.

CHAPTER 16

God Confirms His Word

A few years back, I started putting some posts on Facebook about certain scriptures, things God was dealing with me about and showing me in scripture. That's when God began to put it on my heart to write a book. I pushed it off, as I said, and gave Him every excuse I could. Then, out of the blue, a very well-read pastor friend of mine, to whom I will forever be grateful for, called me to discuss a post I had posted on Facebook, and to commend me for how well written it was. It meant a great deal to get a compliment, especially from him. He went on to ask if I had ever thought about writing a book and told me that I should. I did not tell him that God had been putting it on my heart to do that very thing. I just played it off like it was a crazy idea because I still thought that it was. Here I was, a hillbilly from a one-horse town in the middle of nowhere, and I've never been anywhere or done anything, I can barely read and definitely can't spell or even write well, so I thought, who am I to do this crazy thing?

Several months later while talking to the same pastor friend, laughing about a conversation I had with a dear old lady in our church, I told him how we were discussing traditions and things we were taught in our churches growing up that weren't necessarily biblical.

I told him the lady's response was," I'm going to tell you what I think, and I don't want you quoting me no scripture either."

I started laughing and said, "Okay, but that's the exact problem, we want what we want, but we don't want to know what the Bible says about it."

Fortunately, this dear lady heard how silly that sounded coming out and realized she would rather be biblical than traditional. This pastor friend and I were chuckling about it, and out of the blue he said to me, "You should put that in your book." I could not believe the possibility of me writing a book was referenced again, and I hadn't told anyone about it.

Recently, I was at a church service and the preacher was talking about some of the writers of the Bible and how it must have seemed crazy to them to write some of the books in the Bible.

Then he said, "What about you, would you write something down if God wanted you to?" I said, "Okay, Lord - I'll start writing."

CHAPTER 17

Heartbreaking Reality
"God's Love Note"

I heard a statistic that only 10 or 12 percent of Christians actually read their Bibles. This breaks my heart, and it makes me understand more as to why our country is in the condition it is. Even more so, the church nationwide is in a sad condition. If this breaks our hearts, I can't imagine how it makes God feel. His Word is so precious. It is His love note to His bride, and she won't even read it.

The Holy Word of God holds the recipe for how life works best, it holds the keys to eternal life. Instructions of the wedding, when it will be, and how to get ready for it, and we won't read it. Jesus gave a parable in Matthew 25: 1-13 about ten virgins waiting on their bridegroom, five wise and five foolish. Five did whatever it took to be ready, and they got to go to the wedding. The other five did not because they weren't ready. We better get ready, church.

Then the kingdom of heaven will be like ten virgins who took their lamps and went to meet the bridegroom. Five of them were foolish, and five were wise. For when the foolish took their lamps, they took no oil with them, but the wise took flasks of oil with their lamps. As the bridegroom was delayed, they all became drowsy and slept. But at midnight there was a cry, 'Here is the bridegroom! Come out to meet him.' Then all those virgins rose and trimmed their lamps. And the foolish said to the wise, 'Give us some of your oil, for our lamps are going out.' But the wise answered, saying, 'Since there will be not enough for us and for you, go rather to the dealers and buy for yourselves.' And while they were going to buy, the bridegroom came, and those who were ready went in with him to the marriage fest, and the door was shut. Afterward the other virgins came also, saying, 'Lord, lord, open to us,' But he answered, 'Truly, I say to you, I do not know you.' Watch therefore, for you know neither the day nor the hour."

CHAPTER 18

Biker Salvation

Very early in our ministry at the church, I had a neighbor that owned a house down the road. He stopped by one night. He didn't live there full time; it was his second home by the Lake of the Ozarks. This man had no church upbringing. He was a Vietnam veteran that was battling Agent Orange and flashbacks from the war. His wife had told him she couldn't take it anymore. She feared for her life because she was unable to snap him out of these episodes he would get caught up in, thinking he was still in the war. He knew that I was a preacher so he stopped by my house one night very distraught, not wanting to live anymore because his wife had kicked him out, and he wanted me to bless him so he could go kill himself. I explained to him that I couldn't do that. I tried to tell him that God loved him and wanted a relationship with him. His reply was that there was no way God could love him with all the things he had done in the service, and in a life of drugs and alcohol that followed for many years and in which he was still living. He felt bad for the things he was guilty of and the harm he had caused people all his life.

We read scripture for hours. I showed him how some of God's main people in the Bible were guilty of murder and all sorts of things, but God still loved them and had a plan for them, and they went on to fulfill big plans for God. God convinced him that night through His word that He loved him, and Jesus died for him and would forgive him of all of his sins and cleanse him from all unrighteousness. 1 John 1:19.

He accepted Christ that night as his Lord and Savior. God healed him from his flashbacks and restored his marriage. It wasn't all overnight, the marriage took a little time. His wife was skeptical, but when she saw what God did for him, there was no denying what had happened.

CHAPTER 19

Biker Baptism

We baptized him at the lake by our house during a cool November. I remember the water being so cold. We talked about him being baptized earlier, but he said he needed some time to get some of his friends there. I asked him not to take too long or the lake would be frozen. He said, with laughter in his voice, that if he could take it, I should be able to as well. I will never forget it.

We were going to do the baptism after church one afternoon. He said his friends were just going to meet us. We were all there, the whole church drove down. As we waited a little bit, I asked if they were for sure coming and he said they were. He had made them promise that they would be there.

About that time, he said that they were coming! I looked up the road but didn't see anyone and asked him how he knew. He replied, "Listen!" Then I could hear a rumble that got louder and louder. Around the corner came a whole group of bikers on some mean looking choppers. I'm not talking about bikers for Christ, these were some rough dudes with their lady friends on the back that looked just as tough. I had never seen anything like it. It looked like a scene out of a movie. He said before we got started, he had some things he wanted to say. They gathered around and he told them that they had all witnessed him live for himself and do what he wanted to do his whole life, but that was the old him. He told them all how he was now saved from his sins. He told them how he had given his heart to the Lord and was going to live for Him from now on. He was not the same man. God had changed him, and he wanted them all to hear it from him and be there to see for themselves.

    We prayed over him, baptized him, and then sang *Amazing Grace*. It was truly one of the most exhilarating moments in my ministry to date. I was able to witness what God was doing in his life and bringing those people there at that moment was surreal. Only God can do these things.

CHAPTER 20

God's Word is Precious

Imagine a big man, a Vietnam Veteran, who was now stumbling with cane in hand due to the Agent Orange exposure and what it had done to his body. We gave him a good study Bible to read, and he came to church one day so excited about something he had read in his Bible. I asked him to start with the gospel of John. I can't remember what the scripture was, but he said it was written just for him! It was one of all our favorites, but he was convinced it was put in there just for him. I explained it was there for all of us, God's word was coming alive to him and changing his life.

One morning shortly thereafter, he came to church a little late. It was raining and cold out, Sunday School had already begun, and I was the teacher. I looked up and saw him out the window moving slowly towards the church across the parking lot with a plastic sack under his arm. As I was teaching, I was wondering what he had wrapped up in the plastic sack. As he came through the front door, took off his coat and hung it up, I teared up as I watched him unwrap his Bible out of the plastic sack. He didn't want to get it wet. It was so precious to him, and life changing. Oh, I pray that we would all hold God's word in that high regard. Most of us would put our Bible's over our heads and run for the door.

CHAPTER 21

Lives are at Stake

It is so crucial that we allow God to write on our hearts. The truth is our lives and the lives of others depend on it. In the 2nd chapter of Philippians, the apostle Paul tells us to work out our own Salvation with fear and trembling. Why? Because right before that it says, *"Every knee will bow, and every tongue confesses that Jesus Christ is Lord."*

In 1 Corinthians 2:3, the apostle Paul told the church at Corinth that he came to them with fear and trembling, not because he was scared of man or of God, but because of what was at stake, their souls! Oh, if we would begin to see the need for God to write on our hearts, His word and compassion for the lost. Oh, how God longs for the day we will let Him write these things on our hearts.

Jeremiah 31:33,34 says, *"I will put My law in their minds and write it on their hearts. I will be their God and they will be My people. No longer will a man teach his neighbor or a man his brother, saying 'know the Lord', Because they will all know Me from the least to the greatest declares the Lord."*

We live in a new time under this new covenant, and God wants to do those very things for you and me if we will just let Him. We must allow the Holy Spirit to teach us and bring all things back to our remembrance. He longs to do it if we would just let Him. We must put the word in our minds and hearts first before He can bring it out. He can bring it about in many such ways according to scripture. He has called us to His Glory & His Excellency, and according to 2 Peter 1:5-7:

"For this very reason, we are to make every effort to supplement [our] faith with virtue, and virtue with knowledge, and knowledge with self-control, and self-control with steadfastness, and steadfastness with godliness, and godliness with brotherly affection, and brotherly affection with love."

We can know Galatians 5:16-19

"But I say, walk by the spirit and not gratify the desires of the flesh. For the desires of the flesh are against the Spirit, and the desires of the Spirit are against the flesh, for these are opposed to each other,

to keep you from doing the things you want to do. But if you are led by the Spirit, you are not under the law."

Galatians 5:22-23

"But the fruit of the Spirit is love, joy, peace, patience, kindness, goodness, faithfulness, gentleness, self-control: against such things there is no law.

Galatians 5:24

"And those who belong to Christ Jesus have crucified the flesh with its passions and desires."

CHAPTER 22

God Wants to Use Us to Minister to Those Who are in Captivity

God is still looking for some Shadrach's, Meshach's, and Abednego's willing to change the world. Some of us grew up in church, grew up on accounts like that in the first few chapters of the book of Daniel, fascinated by those three Hebrew boys and what God had done for them in the fiery furnace.

One day, I was reading through the account in Daniel again. I was going to talk to the youth about it that night at church, and I'll never forget it. As I was reading about their faithfulness to God, it seemed like in each chapter God continued to promote them. I remember kind of chuckling and thinking this could be a good prosperity sermon. I am not a prosperity preacher, but God checked me in my spirit and I had the following conversation:

God Wants to Use Us to Minister to Those Who are in Captivity

He asked me. *"You know why I promoted them, don't you?"* My thought was they did not bow to the false god. I remember God replied, *"Yeah, but not really,"* so I said, "They didn't eat the meat offered to idols?" Again, God said, *"Yeah, but not really."* So, I said," No, I guess I don't know. "God's response was, *"I promoted them to better minister to those that were in captivity."*

Wow. That blew me away. It all made perfect sense. Most of the things we go through and learn from aren't just for us or about us, but for someone else. Everything they went through, every test passed, every promotion - was so God could elevate them in Babylon to take care of the rest of His people stuck there in captivity or slavery.

You see, the promotions we have received and the ones we have coming might very well have as much to do with those around us as they do with us. God wants to promote us to better take care of those in captivity around us. I've had to learn that people are more important than my problems. There is always a bigger picture.

CHAPTER 23

Experience God

I remember hearing a preacher say, a long time ago even before I was saved, that a person with an argument doesn't hold a candlestick to one with an experience.

I pray we Experience God, people! I pray we Experience the Power of His Life Changing Word and the revelation it can bring in our lives, of Him, and His great love for us and others around us.

God has been pursuing us our entire lives. Acts 17:27 tells us, He is not far from us.

"...that they should seek God, and perhaps feel their way toward him and find him. Yet he is actually not far from each one of us..."

In the old covenant, God wrote His laws on stone and they were placed in the Ark of the Covenant that Moses had made. That Ark represented God's presence, and it was kept in the temple. In the new covenant, we are the temple of the Holy Spirit, and God wants to write on our hearts and fill our lives with His presence, not just a building.

1 Corinthians 3:16 *"Do you not know that you are God's temple and that God's Spirit dwells in you?"*

We were created for a relationship with Him.

While in the Garden of Eden, Adam and Eve sinned, and God went and found them, He pursued them. God made a sacrifice that covered their sins, and I'm sure God wrote something on their hearts that day. God prepared a sacrifice for you and me. It was His Son Jesus Christ, (the only way by which man can be saved). He is searching out each and every one of us. Can you hear Him calling, coming? Let's not hide, we can't anyway. Let's accept what He has done for us and receive the salvation offered through faith in Jesus Christ.

If you never have, I pray you do today. He will change your life eternally just as in John chapter 11 when Christ called out to Lazarus to come forth. The dead came to life and came out of that dark hole in the ground, then Jesus said, *Loose him* in verse 44.

"The man who had died came out, his hands and feet bound with linen strips, and his face wrapped with a cloth. Jesus said to them, "unbind him, and let him go."

You see they had to unwrap him and take the grave clothes off. Sometimes we have to be loosed and set free from our grave clothes, those garments of the flesh and let Christ resurrect a new man in us to live for Him.

CHAPTER 24

Choose Life

"Here I Am! I stand at the door and knock. If anyone hears My voice and opens the door, I will come in and eat with him and he with Me." Revelation 3:20

Jesus stands at our heart's door knocking, calling out, and desiring to come in. Will you let Him in today? He won't come in unwelcomed. We have to make the choice to let Him in.

Deuteronomy 30:19 says, *"I call heaven and earth to witness against you today, that I have set before you life and death, blessing and curse. Therefore, choose life, that you and your offspring may live…"*

I have chosen so many destructive things in my life, but I'm glad that God has, does, and will forgive me of all of them if I will repent and confess. He will forgive me and cleanse me from all unrighteousness, and He continues to give me the chance to choose life. It is so encouraging to know scripture says not only me, but my children may live.

Our sin doesn't just affect us, but all those under and around us as well. In the same way, when we choose life, the life that comes from faith and trust in Jesus Christ, our lives should positively affect people around us for the good. Let us open our heart's door to Him today. I pray if you never have done this, then let Jesus come in and change your life forever. I pray that you will choose Him, so that you and yours may live.

CHAPTER 25

God Has Plans for You

God uses imperfect people to do His Good and Perfect Will. We are all imperfect, but He can use us. King David was one of those imperfect people that God chose to do great and mighty things through. Even though David was guilty of a lot of things including adultery, murder, lying, and pride, God chose David. Even though David made several poor decisions and even caused thousands of people to die, God forgave him and used him anyway.

1 Chronicles chapter 17, King David wanted to build a permanent house for God. We know that David wasn't the one who was called to the task, but God told David He wanted to build him a house. Oh, what God wants to do for His people, and for you.

Jeremiah 29:11 *"For I know the plans I have for you, declares the Lord. Plans to prosper you and not to harm you, plans to give you hope and a future."*

This was written and sent to those who were in captivity in Babylon. These were people who were stuck in the consequences of their sin. This was during their darkest hour at that time, and God sent them that promise. Wow! You may be stuck in a dark place right now in your life, but you need to know that God has plans for you. God does not want to harm you but to give you hope and a future. It only comes through His son and the forgiveness already paid for you.

Isaiah 40:31 says, "But those that hope in the Lord, will renew their strength. They will soar on wings like eagles. They will run and not grow weary. They will walk and not faint."

Isaiah was prophesying 100 plus years before to the same people that Jeremiah was ministering to. Those who would want to leave Babylonian captivity after the 70 years were accomplished. God promised them that if they would leave the land of bondage, He would give them strength. He said that they would run and not grow weary, walk and not faint. They would mount up on wings like eagles. He still keeps His promises, if you want to leave your Babylon, now is the time. If you are done with your previous life, He will give you a new one: a new outlook, a new vision, a new revelation, a direction and a purpose.

CHAPTER 26

Changed Heart

I am so thankful for all that God has taught me and the changing He has done in my life. He has brought me out of captivity, through His word, and helped those in captivity around me who are in my circle of influence.

Earlier in this book, I made mention about the church I was pastoring being very small in a small town. It was an impoverished community. I remember in the early days of pastoring, it was difficult to see visitors come into the church and not stay. I often wondered if it was because of our few numbers who happened to also be impoverished. Unfortunately, churches need monetary funds to operate and pay bills like everything else in our American culture.

It was difficult to make ends meet, but God was always faithful. I was tired and down in the dumps at one point, and I read through the scriptures in Luke Chapter 7 where John the Baptist sent the disciples to Jesus to ask if He was the One or should they look for another. Jesus told them to go back and tell John what they had seen. Blind eyes were suddenly opened, lame men walked, lepers were cured, deaf could hear again, dead were raised to life, and the poor had the gospel delivered to them.

Luke 7:22, *"And he answered them, 'Go and tell John what you have seen and heard: the blind receive their sight, the lame walk, lepers are cleansed, and the deaf hear, the dead are raised up, the poor have good news preached to them.'"*

Wow! He threw that in with the most miraculous things He was doing. God let me know I was exactly where I was supposed to be. You see, it's nothing short of miraculous when God changes the hearts of men and causes them to love others, especially those not like themselves.

CHAPTER 27

God Alters the Universe for Man

I remember a sermon I preached one time out of Joshua Chapter 10. It was when Joshua and all of Israel went on to fight against five Amorite kings and all their armies. Joshua prayed to the Lord to make the sun stand still over Gibeon and the moon also stand still over the Valley of Aijalon, because if God would, they would finish the fight. God killed more people that day with hailstones than died by the sword. I'm so glad that God didn't tell Joshua that what he was asking was impossible. I mean, think about it. The earth spins over 1000 mph on its axis and travels over 66,000 mph through space. It is crazy to think about, but God stopped it in its tracks for them to have victory over their enemy.

As I was preparing for the sermon, it was like God spoke to me and said the miracle wasn't that He had done that for man, but that man lined his will up with God's will and wanted to do whatever it took to have total victory over his enemies. Wow! To think that

God would alter the universe for me and not just that, but would give His Son to come to this earth and die for us and pay our sin debt. Then God raised Him from the dead so we could have life and be victorious over all our enemies. You see, the miracle isn't that God can change the universe, of course He can, but what's more miraculous is He can change us, if we let Him, if you let Him. We can change our world through Him. People need to see this life changing power in our lives. All of our lives depend on it.

CHAPTER 28

God Gives Us a New Heart to Worship

We had other issues going on in our little church other than lower socioeconomic status of those attending and an underlying barrier present. Our worship was less than mediocre. My wife nor I played any instruments nor did we sing, so we were no help. When no one in the church was really called to do it, we were kind of stuck with whoever would fill the need. One could only imagine how it was, to say the least, it was less than mediocre.

Typically, worship sets the stage for the sermon to follow, and I had to follow the less than enthusiastic worship service, so this was really difficult for me to get my heart and mind prepared. This was especially difficult since my wife and I had come from a church with awesome, I mean outstanding praise and worship. The pastor's wife was the worship leader then, and I thought she was the most anointed worship leader I've ever been around. Being called out of a church with incredible praise and worship to go and pastor a church of less than ten in the congregation with no praise and worship to speak of, just hymns and an out of tune piano, you can only imagine my dismay. To make things worse, the song leader didn't even take it seriously. It was rough to say the least.

    It was about a year or year and a half into my pastoring at the little church when I couldn't take it anymore. I remember sitting on the platform trying to keep my thoughts together before preaching. Things were exceptionally bad that particular morning. I remember telling God that I couldn't do it anymore and I was sorry, but I was going to resign.

He then spoke something into my spirit that changed my life.

    He said, *"You know it's a shame that you think you have to have good musicians and people that sing in the same key before you think you can worship Me."*

Ouch! I began to weep so hard before the Lord and I repented. I knew we should worship Him for who He is and what He has done in our lives and because He is worthy. You see, we almost have to ask ourselves, "If I can only enter in and worship when a popular song is playing or when there is smoke and lights to go with the awesome music, "just what are we worshipping?" Don't get me wrong, I do like all of that, but something is wrong when we can't worship without it. If you will worship Him for who He is and realize He is worthy even if everything isn't perfect and they aren't singing your favorite song, you won't ever have another dry worship service. I know I haven't.

CHAPTER 29

God Changes Our Perspective

Habakkuk was a great example, from who we can learn. He took his complaints to God and did not really like the answers God gave him. However, he continued to go back and forth with God until God changed his heart and attitude. It was not necessarily the circumstances that changed, but rather his outlook. We can find an example in Habakkuk 3: 17 -19 as it gives us an awesome look at how Habakkuk's mindset changed. Habakkuk penned these life changing scriptures that only God had written on his heart.

Verse 17-19 says, *"Though the fig tree does not bud, and there are no grapes on the vines, though the olive crop fails, and the fields produce no food. Though there be no sheep in the pen and no cattle in the stalls. I will rejoice in the Lord; I will be joyful in God my savior. The sovereign Lord is my strength. He makes my feet like the feet of a deer. He enables me to go on the Heights."*

When I write about Heart Ink, this is a prime example of what I mean, its life changing, inscripted Word written on our hearts. It changes us forever.

CHAPTER 30

True Heart Ink

S ometimes we think that God has written things on our hearts because we have memorized scripture perhaps when we went to church camp, from Sunday School, or just from self-study, but that's not true Heart Ink. God showed me that sometimes we don't truly believe a promise until that promise is all we have to get us through.

My wife and I wanted to have kids right away, after we got married. Unfortunately, she couldn't conceive at that time. There were a lot of things going on in her body that were working against her getting pregnant. She had polycystic ovarian syndrome along with other complications, but we believed God was our Healer. He was and is the Giver and Keeper of life. We knew He could allow us to have kids, it was not impossible.

We also believed God gave doctors knowledge to help His people. We were going to a specialist and doing everything they said. We were about 7 years into trying everything, so we finally saved enough money to have In Vitro Fertilization done. One can imagine how excited we were to learn the procedure had been successful. She was pregnant. All our prayers for years, prayers from all our family members were answered. We just believed if God wanted to use In Vitro, then it was fine with us. We struggled over seven years of dealing with why of this happening to us when we wanted children. We could not understand why it could happen for everyone else, even those who did not even want children, but it could not happen for us. We had all of the emotions a couple normally has when struggling to conceive. We were glad it was all over, and it finally happened.

Soon thereafter, we got a call from the doctor's office indicating they had seen something abnormal in Melissa's blood levels. The numbers weren't climbing like they should. We had been elated over the exciting news and were told we could tell everyone. Then suddenly, we were informed Melissa would most likely miscarry. We were heartbroken to say the least. We were informed it would take several days, they weren't 100 percent sure yet, but that's what they feared was going to happen. We prayed so hard. They wanted to take blood a couple more times to be sure. It took about a week to determine what was really happening, and it felt like the longest week of our lives. Unfortunately, it was true, Melissa had miscarried.

I like to think of myself as a pretty practical person and not much catches me off guard, but this really blindsided me. The thought of miscarrying had never even entered my mind. Worse yet, was that it hurt so much because I knew God had allowed it. I felt God was playing with our emotions. At first, I thought God let the In Vitro work and we trusted Him to use that, but then He allowed this to happen. I was deeply wounded. I was at work when Melissa called and told me what the doctor's office said. It was clear, they were 100 percent certain. I cried so hard and was really giving God a piece of my mind. I told Him I was resigning from the church and was done. I don't remember everything I said, but I said I was done and I told Him that multiple times. He let me go on for quite a while then He spoke Romans 8:28 to me in this way.

> *"In all things I work for the good of those who love Me and are called according to My purpose."* Then He said, *"Do you believe this?"* I told Him that I used to! He replied, *"That's not what I asked, I asked if you believe it. Because if you don't believe it then you are right, we are done. Because I can't help you if you don't believe My word and My promises."*

You see, I only thought I believed God's promise in Romans 8:28 until it became essential that I did believe the promise to get through what I was facing. Even when I didn't understand it all, I believed the promise and my faith in that promise got me through.

God knew six months later Melissa would get pregnant on her own, but I didn't. We would then go on to have two more beautiful kids. Sometimes He does things we cannot see or understand because He has a much greater plan. Until that time, understanding *"all things work for the good of those who love Me and are called according to My purpose,"* were merely words on a page.

After that, they finally became a part of who I am today. Those words were no longer just the Apostle Paul's revelation, but now they were mine too. God wants *"all things to work for your good"* too, and give you every other promise ever written in His word.

CHAPTER 31

Faith Don't Fail Us Now

We must believe His promises. Our faith in Him is crucial. In Luke 22:31-32 Jesus told Simon Peter that Satan's desire was to sift him like wheat, not flour, but wheat.

"Simon, Simon, behold, Satan demanded to have you, that he might sift you like wheat, but I have prayed for you that your faith may not fail."

To sift wheat, the farmer would pick the stalks up, beat them repeatedly on the ground, then shake them violently. Then they do it all again. Finally, they would roll the wheat around under their feet to separate it from the skin, scoop it up, and toss it to the wind so the shaft could be blown away.

I am sure most of us can relate to this. It feels like the enemy does this to all of us all of the time. How comforting it is to know that Jesus is praying for us and that our faith doesn't fail! Jesus didn't tell Simon Peter that the devil was going to take it easy on him. However, he gave us encouragement through the following verse.

He said, *"I've prayed for you that your faith doesn't fail." (V.32).*

My prayer is that we all know how important our faith in God is, and our faith in what He has done for us through His Son Jesus Christ. It is His word that He wants to write on our hearts that will eternally change our lives if we will allow it.

In John 8:31, 32 Jesus said, *"If you abide in my word, you are truly my disciples, and you will know the truth, and the truth will set you free."*

You see, we have to hold to it, and know it. Then it will set us free.

CHAPTER 32

God Does See, He is Here

I don't recommend throwing a tantrum with God or giving Him what-for, but God is big enough to handle it. I think He would rather have us come to Him and throw a fit, be honest and real with Him, than just leave and not talk to Him again.

Job was a man of God who gave some great insight into this. The Bible says Job was a righteous man and rich. It also tells of how he lost almost everything in one day. He lost his kids, crops, livestock, servants, all in the same day. Then he lost his health and the respect of friends and his wife. People accused him of some hidden sin that caused all that to happen to him. Although he maintained his innocence, things started getting to Job.

Job Chapter 23 tells us how Job complained and he was bitter. If he knew where to find God, he would go to Him and make his case before God. He knew God would not oppose him, but rather listen. Job went on to say how he couldn't see God in his problems. He couldn't sense Him anywhere, whether He was before or behind him, to the right or to the left. Following this paragraph, Job delivered a profound statement of faith.

"But he knows the way that I take; when he has tried me, I shall come out as gold." (V.10)

Many have heard about the patience of Job, but let's consider the faith of Job. Although Job couldn't see or sense God in all his problems, at least Job knew God was with him.

We need to know He sees us, He knows. He knows exactly where we are at and exactly what to do. We are going to come forth like gold. Let's hang in there.

CHAPTER 33

You Can Be Emotional, But Don't Doubt

I have learned that being upset about something isn't always a lack of faith. I was heavily convicted when I noticed something in Jeremiah about a couple of his prayers. In Chapter 15, Jeremiah prayed and sought earnestly as many of the faith have at some point during their lives.

Jeremiah 15: 15-18

"O LORD, you know: remember me and visit me, and take vengeance for me on my persecutors. In your forbearance take me not away; know that for your sake I bear reproach. Your words were found, and I ate them, and your words became to me a joy and a delight of my heart, for I am called by your name, O LORD, God of hosts. I did not set in the company of revelers nor did I rejoice; I sat alone, because your hand was upon me, for you had filled me with indignation. Why is my pain unceasing, my wound incurable,

refusing to be healed? Will you be to me like a deceitful brook, like waters that fail?"

Jeremiah went on in Chapter 20 and prayed things none of us would want to go on record for praying.

"O LORD, you have deceived me, and I was deceived; you are stronger than I, and you have prevailed. I have become a laughingstock all the day; everyone mocks me. For whenever I speak, I cry out, I shout, 'Violence and destruction!' for the word of the LORD has become for me a reproach and derision all day long." (V.7-8)

He just poured out his frustrations to God indicating every bad thing that happened to him was because of God and he considered not speaking in The Lord's name anymore.

It was shocking to me when I noticed the prayer God demanded he repent for praying. It was the prayer in

Jeremiah 15:19 *"Therefore this is what the Lord says: "if you repent, I will restore you that you may serve Me; if you utter worthy, not worthless, words, you will be My spokesman. Let this people turn to you, but you must not turn to them."*

You Can Be Emotional, But Don't Doubt

You see the prayer in Chapter 20 was real. It was how he was feeling and all his emotions were real to him, he genuinely felt that way although he was emotional and upset. It wasn't really a prayer of unbelief or doubt. The prayer in Chapter 15, though the words were written more eloquently so as not to offend as much, it actually offended God more. He demanded him to repent thinking God may not come through. It wasn't like He couldn't restore or couldn't solve his incurable wound. We must not pray in doubt. We all need to repent sometimes of the way we pray. Jeremiah Chapter 20 went on to say in Verse 9,

"He couldn't stop speaking for God because His word was like fire shut up in his bones. He couldn't hold it in."

How amazing it could be if we would allow God's word to set us on fire from the inside out! What could we accomplish for God? Hebrews Chapter 11, the great chapter of faith, reminds us of this in Verse 6.

"And without faith it is impossible to please him, for whoever would draw near to God must believe that he exists and that he rewards those who seek him."

It tells us that it is impossible to please God without faith, and that if anyone comes to Him, he must believe that He is, and that He is a rewarder of those that diligently seek Him. God is big enough to handle our emotions, but still wants our faith. He understands we won't always like our circumstances, but we must believe He is bigger than our circumstances.

CHAPTER 34

Thank You, Men and Women of God

It Starts With Us

I know I am just one person on this globe in the enormous universe in which we live. God has holy men and women all over this nation and globe. He has been writing on their hearts for many years, great ministries have been founded, lives have been saved, and love has been given to mankind because of their faithfulness. They have been making a difference in the Kingdom of God ever since they received their Heart Ink. I wish to thank them for their services and encourage them to keep making a difference.

 I know we all wonder why we go through some of the things we do at times. I know we have learned over the years that it is so we can help others later. God wants men and women of vision that are okay with going through hard things at times, if it means it will help others that don't have a relationship yet with the Lord. They will if we hang in there. Apostle Paul often said that what he went through- he did it for them.

I pray you allow God to write on your hearts to make you the best able-bodied minister that you can be to whomever you minister. We all have people in our circle of influence. We can read 2 Chronicles 7:14 and be reminded,

"If My people, who are called by My name, will humble themselves and pray, and seek My face and turn from their wicked ways, then will I hear from heaven and will forgive their sin and heal their land."

Did you see the part, "If My people"? This is what I pray we all understand.

If it can't start with each and every one of us, the church, Saints of God, believers, then how will it ever happen for the unbelievers? He longs to forgive our sins and heal our land; He is waiting on us to do our part. I pray we do not perish for a lack of wisdom, vision, revelation, or heart ink.

Hebrews 12:2, *"Let us fix our eyes on Jesus, the founder (author) and perfecter (finisher) of our faith…"*

CHAPTER 35

The Word Became Flesh

If we really want God to write His Word on our hearts, we need to fall in love with His Word - which means we are to fall in love with Him.

John 1:1,2 says, *"In the beginning was the Word and the Word was with God and the Word was God." Verse 2, "He was with God in the beginning."*

In *1:14 it says, "The Word became flesh and made His dwelling among us we have seen His glory, the glory of the One and only Son who came from the Father, full of grace and truth."*

"Jesus became flesh and dwelt among us." The Greek word for *word* is logos. Our definition for logos is the embodiment of a thought or an idea. God's Word is His concrete thought process towards us. It's His mindset, His love note to us, His creation.

CHAPTER 36

A Good Understanding of the Old Testament Will Give You a Better Understanding of the New Testament

For a long time, I didn't read a lot in the Old Testament. I would read it, but I did most of my teaching and preaching from the New Testament. While there is nothing wrong with focusing on the New Testament, I realized it's all God's Word. The more I learned about the Old Testament I got intrigued by it, and it started coming alive to me. It was amazing how learning the Old Testament shed a new light on the New Testament. The Old Testament used to be the only Bible there was. The disciples referenced the Old Testament throughout, and it all pointed to Christ. Everything points directly to Christ, every single Old Testament prophesy, and all was fulfilled in the New Testament. It was overwhelming for me to see and understand how God used the prophets to point to Christ.

Unfortunately, the people of His day missed it for the most part. He was right there, walking among men of that day, and they completely missed the Messiah. I know it's easy for us to understand that now since we live in the present. The past can show how dangerous religion and preconceived ideas of what we think God's Word says can be. It can cause us to miss what it's saying completely. When we allow preconceived ideas of what God's word says to keep us from seeing its true meaning, we miss out on many blessings because of it. I do not claim to be a scholar by any means, but it's hard for me not to preach Christ from the Old Testament and tie it into the New Testament because it helps it make more sense a lot of times.

      One thing that helped me understand was that I began to pay attention to the dates. I began to understand when some of the main things happened in the Old Testament. For example, the fall of Jerusalem that occurred in 586 BC give or take, which wasn't the start of the 70 years of Babylonian captivity. It actually started about 11 years before then.

      The book of Jeremiah becomes easier to understand when we realize most all of his ministry was just before and during the reign of Nebuchadnezzar, King of Babylon, when they gained control of that part of the world. We learn that God used Nebuchadnezzar to discipline His people.

      Isaiah came alive for me when I realized it was primarily two different books. Chapters 1 through 39 were written dealing with the people and the kings that were in power during Isaiah's time. Chapters 40 through 66 were written prophetically to those that would be in and coming out of the 70-year Babylonian captivity.

Isaiah's ministry was mainly over almost 100 years before the Babylonian captivity ever happened. God used Isaiah to give His people promise after promise of how He would bring them home, restore the land, and establish them as God's people again. God even called Cyrus by name about 150 years before he conquered Babylon and let God's people go free. Cyrus prefigured Christ. God even called him His Shepherd, and His anointed one.

In the essence he was the Warrior King, the deliverer, which defeated the enemy with no help from God's people. He provided all they needed to go home and be God's people. Cyrus provided military escorts, money, and even gave them all the articles of the temple back that had been taken. All they had to do was want it for themselves and go. That's exactly what Christ did for us. He came to us fulfilling prophecy as God's anointed. He fought for us. He paid for our sins so we could come home and be God's people. Christ is our Warrior King.

When we read up on some history, I want to encourage you to pay attention to the dates in the Bible as it really helps understand the minds and hearts of the people in that time. It helps to clarify what the writers might have been saying and how it might have been received by the people.

It is also noteworthy to realize that some of Israel's darkest times spiritually came during or after their most prosperous times because they took their eyes off of God.

Thank You, God, for Your long-suffering nature and forgiveness of sin and Your unfailing love for Your people.

When reading through Isaiah, it's easy to see why it's considered the most referenced Old Testament book in the New Testament.

CHAPTER 37

It All Points To Christ

It was fascinating for me to understand the Feasts of Israel were to be Holy convocations, rehearsals if you will, they looked forward to something. There were so many things that surround these feasts that pointed to Christ that just blew me away, as I am sure they will you. When we begin to understand these, we understand New Testament scripture in a whole new light. For example, when I re-read statements John the Baptist gave about Jesus being the Lamb of God that takes away the sins of the world, I noticed the day and hour in which Jesus died. I began to notice details of things said around and from the cross. Psalms 22 is a complete word picture of what was going to happen at Calvary. It is fascinating that the description of exactly what would happen at Calvary was written long before Christ was born.

Another fact I find interesting can be found in the longest chapter of the Bible. Psalm 119 describes someone elaborating in great detail how awesome God's Word is, and what it is doing for us.

Ezekiel and Daniel were prophets who wrote from Babylon. What an encouragement to know and understand how even during their darkest hour, God had not forgotten them, rather, He placed people with them to continue to give them His word and minister to them through the tough times.

CHAPTER 38

Judgement Begins With Us

We, as God's people need to realize that judgment begins in the House of God. It starts with us. We need to realize this before we pass judgment on others.

Ezekiel 9:6, *"Kill old men outright, young men and maidens, little children and women, but touch no one on whom is the mark. And begin at my sanctuary."* So they began with the elders who were before the house.

1 Peter 4:17, *"For it is time for judgment to begin at the household of God; and if it begins with use, what will be the outcome for those who do not obey the gospel of God?"*

I remember a time when reading through Luke Chapter 9. It was the account when Jesus fed the 5,000. Before this, He told His disciples to find a way to feed them, but they did not understand how. They didn't understand how they could possibly feed so many with so little, so He showed them. Likewise, near the end of the chapter while the disciples were preparing to pass through Samaria, the Samaritans opposed them and wouldn't let them stay because they were just passing through headed for Jerusalem.

Some of the disciples wanted to know if Jesus wanted them to call fire down from heaven upon the town. Thankfully, Jesus rebuked them and wouldn't allow this. I found it ironic that we often don't have the faith to feed the hungry or minister to the hurting around us, but we seem to find the faith to try to call fire down on people that oppose us. I pray God helps us to see mankind through His eyes and love on them with the love and compassion with which He loves us.

CHAPTER 39

From the Gates of Hell to the Front Pew God's Word is the Same

There are several scriptures indicating how God is the Potter and we, His people, are the clay. Jeremiah 18:6b details this: *"Behold, like the clay in the potter's hand, so are you in my hand, O house of Israel." (V.6b)*

Interestingly, immediately following the potter and clay message, Jeremiah 19 tells of how God told Jeremiah to go to the potter's house and buy a clay jar.

"Thus says the LORD, 'Go, buy a potter's earthenware flask'..." (V.1a)

I don't know if it was the same potter and the same vessel he watched being made in Chapter 18 or not, but he was told to go buy one.

Then he was told to take some elders and priests along with him and go down to the Potsherd gate which was an entrance into the

Valley of Ben Hinnom. This was profound because the Valley of Ben Hinnom was the same as the Valley of Gehenna, which was where we get the word *hell*. It was the city dump; it was the valley they sacrificed their children to the false god Molech. Dead bodies and ashes were dumped there. That's why they said it was a place where the worm or maggot dies not.

Mark 9:43-44, *"If your hand causes you to sin, cut it off. It is better for you to enter life crippled than with two hands to go to hell, into the fire that shall never be quenched where 'their worm does not die and fire is not quenched'."*

There was constant fire, smell, and stench of death, along with broken and unfixable vessels. That's why they metaphorically use this place to refer to hell.

Jeremiah took the people to see for themselves, it was "from the gates of hell so to speak," he begged them to repent before it was too late. What a compassionate God we have, to think that He continues to call out to us right up until it's too late… He wants all to come to know Him.

Just as interesting was when Jeremiah left the Potsherd gate, he went straight to the temple with the same message; "Repent, seek God." It's true, He is the only One that can help us get through. Sadly, God had to bring judgment upon them. He said He would because in the last verse He said they would not listen to His word.

Jeremiah 19:15, *"Thus says the LORD of hosts, the God of Israel, behold, I'm bringing upon this city and upon all its towns all the disaster that I have pronounced against it, because they have stiffened their neck, refusing to hear my words."*

It would be unfortunate to bypass the blessings we could receive because of our lack of Heart Ink and understanding of God's word.

CHAPTER 40

Neat to Think About

The more I've studied, the more I've realized there are some neat things in Jewish tradition or in their Targum, that I find exciting to think about. The Targum is a collection of Jewish writings of Jewish history and oral traditions passed down through the ages.

There are a few things I'd like to share with you. They aren't necessarily written in the scriptures we have today, rather an oral tradition of the Jewish people is this: the first tablets of the Ten Commandments Moses threw down and broke were placed in the Ark of the Covenant as well as the new ones. When I thought of the commandments I have broken and my broken life, I was astounded at how I could be accepted, useful, and desired when I was brought in under the blood of Jesus and began living in the presence of God.

Further, Golgotha means the place of the skull. I believe there are many different reasons why we believe the place Jesus died was called this. Goah was mentioned in Jeremiah 31:39 from which Golgotha was derived.

Jewish tradition orally passed down through the ages said Noah had taken the bones and the skull of Adam on the ark with them. Afterwards, he commanded one of his sons to go bury it in the center of the Earth. Golgotha was where they believed his skull and bones were buried for hundreds of years before Christ.

Although not found in scripture, based on God's character, it sounds like something He would do. He would think to have the second Adam (Jesus) die and have His blood which was shed for the sins of the entire world drop to the ground in the very spot of the first Adam, who caused sin and death to enter His world, and where the last bit of his remains were laid to rest.

To think, Jesus would pay for what Adam did in the very spot he lay, and redeem him and everyone else that believes from the cause and effect of our own sin. Only God could orchestrate something like that.

These things are not just made up by Christians, for the Jewish people believed this all true as well. How splendid just to think it could be a possibility is truly awesome. It was overwhelming to me to think of all the details and orchestrations God did trying to get us to recognize Him and His Son, Jesus, and to recognize Him for who He is.

CHAPTER 41

Definitions Change Everything

When I began to look up meanings and definitions of words, it really helped things come to life for me, and I hope it does for you as well.

Earlier, when Jeremiah 31:33 was mentioned, right after God said He wanted to write His word on our hearts, God gave us some promises about what would happen if we allowed Him to do that.

Jeremiah 31: 35 – 37 says, "For *this is what the Lord says, He who appoints the sun to shine by day, who decrees the moon and stars to shine by night. Who stirs up the sea so that its waves roar? The Lord almighty is His name: only if these decrees vanish from My site, declares the Lord, will the descendants of Israel ever cease to be a nation before Me.*

This is what the Lord says: only if the heavens above could be measured and the foundations of the earth below be searched out will I reject all the descendants of Israel because of all they have done. Declares the Lord."

Wow! God was saying He will never stop loving us. If the sun is up or the moon and stars are out over you right now, God loves you and you will never stop being His. Even after research and study, scientists today still can't map out the oceans or know all that's under the sea. The heavens cannot be measured. God knew it could not be done; He will never stop pursuing us to be His.

While studying Verses 38-40, was when I stumbled across the Jewish tradition of Adam's skull. I was studying and preaching through the book of Jeremiah when I found many of the chapters to be awesome. However, Chapter 31 was really resonating with my soul. I remember getting to the end of the chapter, Verses 38-40.

"The days are coming declares the Lord, when this city will be rebuilt for Me from the tower of Hananel to the Corner Gate. The measuring line will stretch from there straight to the hill of Gareb and then turn to Goah. The whole valley where dead bodies and ashes are thrown, and all the terraces out to the Kidron Valley on the East as far as the corner of the horse gate will be holy to the Lord. The city will never again be uprooted or demolished."

These are the oracles of God, let us take note, rejoice and be made full in Him. Only He can complete us. He is our maker.

CHAPTER 42

Ask God to Open Your Understanding

I remember praying and asking God what this was saying. When we read words like" the days are coming", it can be determined something exciting should happen soon. The entire chapter was prophetic about restoration, God's unfailing love, and His desire to write His word on our hearts. When I think I'm missing something that's right in front of me, I have learned to dig deeper, look at definitions of the word, and analyze, then and only then do things start coming together for me. God is so big, I am sure I miss a lot, but God said He was going to start with the Tower of Hananel: which means God is gracious, or favor. The wall was going to begin/ flow from His grace. It all starts there, with His grace - to Gareb: means scabby or scrape. The reason was because it was where the lepers were pushed outside the city. Since they were covered in leprosy, they had to live separated from the rest of the people. Then on to GOAH, the place of the skull or mount of execution. (Golgotha) or (Calvary) then on to Gehenna, the valley of death (Hell), then to Kidron Valley, which was full of tombs, sepulchers, bones of the dead like the city cemetery another sign or symbol of death. Then on to the Horse Gate: stables and symbols of workers, travel and humanity.

God was saying He longed for the day to expand the wall and boundaries to take in all that had been shunned and pushed away because of disease or sin riddled lives, the spiritually dead and bound for hell, all humanity -He longs to save us. He longs to have relationships with us and it all flows to us from His Grace. Wow.

CHAPTER 43

Royal Priesthood

God said in Verse 40 all these things normally deemed unclean were going to be holy to the Lord. He used the same terminology for the priests and utensils used in the service of God performed in the temple. Holy, devoted to God. Wow! It is overwhelming to think that because of the grace and love of God that flows to us through His son Jesus Christ, I can be forgiven and cleansed of all unrighteousness. I can become the righteousness of God through Christ Jesus.

God wants us to be holy devoted to Him by the sanctifying work of the Holy Spirit. It doesn't matter who we are or what we've done, God chooses *us*. God's Word explains how everything used in worship was to be holy unto the Lord. The high priest was to be anointed with a special holy anointing oil. God gave Moses the recipe and told him that there was not to be any replacements or any other like it. What a great parallel for understanding there is no substitute for the anointing of the Holy Spirit in our lives. There is no substitute for God being the One to teach us and **write something on your hearts**.

"By Grace through faith are we saved." Ephesians 2:8-9.

God doesn't want to exclude any but wants all to be saved, He wants all to have **Heart Ink**. His desire is for us to be changed and eternally inked by the Creator Himself.

CHAPTER 44

Let the River Flow

Jeremiah 31:38-40 also reminded me of Ezekiel's vision in Chapter 47 about the water flowing from the temple. It kept flowing East, East, East. He asked Ezekiel if he had seen this. The water or the Word, the Spirit of God, that flows from God to the East. Here is an example of when I took my study further. I looked at my maps, and saw the Dead Sea and the Arabian Desert being the most desolate and dry areas in the land, yet that's precisely where His spirit was flowing.

God wants nothing more than to flow into the dead dry places of our lives and heal those areas. He wants to bring life and restoration back into the hearts of us that have kept Him pushed out way too long. Let's allow Him into every area of your lives today, let's allow God to continue to write our stories. Let's allow His Holy Word to penetrate deep down into our lives. Let's allow Him to call us out deeper and deeper until there is water to swim.

Ezekiel 47: 5 *"He measured off another thousand cubits, but now it was a river that I could not cross, because the water had risen and was deep enough to swim in—a river that no one could cross."*

There are deeper things out there for us people, deep things of God, an endless supply of His wisdom, knowledge, grace, love, forgiveness, peace, and joy. It's yours if you want it.

    I don't consider myself to be long winded, as I've considered this book, Heart Ink. I've oftentimes thought that one of the hardest things about preaching was knowing what not to say. I cipher what material to leave out and still get the point across. I realize everyone is different and some messages do take longer but knowing when to stop and let God do the rest is sometimes hard. I pray God does what He needs to do in all of our lives.

My Prayer

Dear God, I pray that I have said and done what You have called me to do. Lord knows I don't understand why, but I know You don't make mistakes. So, I trust someone, somewhere, at some point will be encouraged by what You have asked me to do. Lord, forgive me for taking so long and for being afraid of failure and anxious of doing the craziest thing to date in my life.

As for our country, I pray You help men and women of faith to get serious about Your word and allowing You to write on their hearts on a daily basis. God, I thank You for every time You've written on our hearts in the middle of our circumstances, but God, I pray that we will start gaining vision and revelation before the trials come, instead of only through them.

Lord, help us not to become complacent in our lives in any area. God, I thank You for every pastor and teacher out there, for the work they do for You and Your Kingdom, but I pray that You become our greatest teacher. I pray we don't believe it because man said it, but Lord, because You have etched it on our hearts. May we fan into flame any and all gifts You have given us so we can make the biggest difference in people's lives that we can, because the days are getting short. Help us to realize what is at stake.

My Prayer

In Jesus name, Amen.

He's just waiting for your cooperation to finish your story, to write on your heart.

"Get Inked."

Heart Ink that is.

Pastor Jason Moppin

Words of Encouragement

The following pages are a collection of some old Facebook posts, I hope you enjoy them. They are just some examples of God revealing His word to me and writing on my heart. Use them as encouragement or devotions and be blessed.

Thank you, to anyone who reads this.

Note: These are raw, unedited, and candid posts, just moments from my heart.

Words of Encouragement

Post #1

A few weeks ago while driving down the road and praying, and feeling very insufficient. I began to tell God remorsefully that I was sorry I didn't bring more to the table. His response was that, it's ok, I couldn't bring enough anyway, because all my trying just belittles my worth, and the price He already payed for me. This really floored me, and puts things into perspective about how valuable we are to God. That you are worth so much more than any amount of human effort or work. That's why we cant do it on our own. Most importantly He also showed us our value to Him when He gave His Son to take our place on the cross at Calvary hence we have been bought with the precious blood of Jesus. I know we are called unto good works, and please do them so man might see our good works and give God the glory, but please know you are worth so much more to God than anything you think you are, or are trying to bring to the table. Don't belittle your worth. We are His. Let's rest in Him.

Post #2

The bible speaks of all of creation praising and worshipping God, and I love that worship song that says "ain't no rock, gonna cry in my place as long as I'm alive to glorify Your holy name". We definitely need to be people of praise. But in the account in the gospel of Luke 19:40 when Christ told the Pharisees if they keep quiet, the stones will cry out. I personally do not believe that He was talking about praise, but judgment. Jesus partially quoted Habakkuk 2:11 as He often did with the Pharisees. He would quote a scripture to them and when you go back and read it in the Old Testament and see what was going on and why the scripture was originally given it speaks volumes into what the Pharisees were doing in Jesus's time. That's why a lot of things He said to them made them so mad because they knew what scripture He was quoting and couldn't believe He could apply that to them. I believe this is one of those times. I don't believe it was a coincidence He used words only used pretty much one time in scripture and it not be a quotation. So when we go back and look in Habakkuk chapter two, God is speaking to Habakkuk about how He will deal the enemies of Gods people. He tells him to mark it down, it will happen. He said though it lingers, wait on it. It is for an appointed time, and would not prove false. God told Habakkuk that the righteous must live by faith. He went on to describe the wickedness of those that would receive this judgment, how they brought shame upon their own house, forfeiting their life. Who builds a city on bloodshed and a town by crime. How their labor was just fuel for the fire, and they exhausted themselves for nothing. It was to these that the stones would cry out against. I know in Habakkuk God was talking about the Babylonians (those that were oppressing Gods people) but it sure sounds like the Pharisees Jesus was speaking to. (And the world today as well) after God said they were exhausting themselves for nothing. After they worked so hard to see their plans through. V14 says THE EARTH WILL BE FILLED WITH THE KNOWLEDGE OF THE GLORY OF THE LORD. Christ preached faith in Him. (The righteous shall live by faith) and those people that were shouting hosanna, hosanna to the highest. They were silenced, they bought into the plans of the Pharisees and were shouting crucify Him just days later, and because they did, and because God raised Him from the grave 3 days later, the whole earth is being filled with the knowledge of the glory of the Lord. Now not all believe but how shall they believe lest they hear. The world would like to silence Gods people today, but we need to be reminded what's at stake if we are. Jesus went on to say in Luke that because they did not recognize what (or Whom) would bring them peace, not one stone would be left upon another. The revelation of Gods judgment in Habakkuk was said to have an appointed. God knows when He is coming, He has it all planned out. We just need to be ready. And that involves repenting, making things right, leaving our gifts on the altar at times and taking care of business. Let's make the most of what time we have left. Be encouraged today, rejoice in the fact that Jesus died for you and rose again so you can have eternal life in Him if you so choose. Choose life. Be blessed in Jesus name. Jason

Post #3
Noticed something in scripture last week that I never had. A phrase caught my attention, now we have all read and heard of king David's

23 Psalm where he describes a valley of the shadow of death. But in Mathew 4:12-17 Mathew quotes a prophecy out of Isaiah 9:1-3 where he describes this certain region of Israel as THE LAND OF THE SHADOW OF DEATH wow the land, that sounds worse than just a valley. That's valley after valley, hill after hill, field after field, the whole land. Now I had never noticed that before so I started digging, and I'm sure there is so much more that I missed, but here is a couple awesome discoveries that excited me, They were the most beat up on tribes in Israel, the farthest north where most all their enemies that destroyed them came from. The farthest away from the temple (the presence of God). Some of the most messed up spiritually, And it's where Jesus made his home and the base of His ministry. Wow, He could have chosen anywhere, but He chose there. And it was wasn't a last second decision either, Isaiah's prophecy was almost 800 years before, and since God knows all things He chose it from the beginning, God has always wanted to go to and minister to the darkest most down and out, farthest away from Him people He can find. He chooses you, He chooses me, He chooses them. In Isaiah it says He went to them to be a great light, enlarge them, increase their joy, cause them to rejoice at the harvest, rejoice like men that rejoice over plunder. Plunder is what they divided up after winning a war or battle. Christ wants to disperse your darkness, make you victorious over your enemies, and enlarge your spiritual life and understanding, give you cause to rejoice over victory and

harvest. If those were Christ targeted people, they should be ours as well Be blessed.

Post #4

Jeremiah 5:30,31. A horrible and shocking thing has happened in the land. The prophets prophesy lies, the priests` rule by their own authority, and my people love it this way. But what will you do in the end? It`s almost hard to believe this was wrote over 2600 years ago and not yesterday

Post #5

In Mathew 9:9 Jesus calls Mathew to come and follow Him. Later they are at Mathews house eating with other tax collectors and " sinners " now the Pharisees and religious leaders didn't like that so they asked the disciples why their teacher would do such a thing.

When Christ heard this, He told them, it's not the healthy that need a doctor, but the sick. Then in verse 13 He says GO AND LEARN WHAT THIS MEANS: I DESIRE MERCY, NOT SACRIFICE. FOR I HAVE NOT COME TO CALL THE RIGHTEOUS, BUT SINNERS. Now of course we all need to learn that but what He really did was quoted part of a scripture out of HOSEA 6:6 and this is where it gets really convicting for us

Christians that must put the Pharisee in ourselves to death every day along with our flesh. When you go back and read in Hosea

Words of Encouragement

Ch.6 around verse 4 God gets onto the children of Israel for their love being so short lived and quickly disappearing. In verse 6 He says, FOR I DESIRE MERCY, NOT SACRIFICE, AND ACKNOWLEDGMENT OF GOD RATHER THAN BURNT OFFERINGS. then He goes on to talk about the men of GILEAD, now Gilead was a place of very fertile ground.

They grew a lot of things there, things they used in their medicines of that day, it was meant to be a place where healing came from. Jeremiah in one of his prophetic words said is there was no balm in Gilead? Is there no physician there? Why then is there no healing for the wound of my people? Jesus is the only remedy for sin, He is the balm of Gilead. But it was supposed to be a place of healing, like our churches should be today, places of healing, and not murder.

When Christ told those Pharisees to go learn what that meant, I'm convinced He wanted them the go read this chapter in Hosea. Verse 8 says this place of healing was a city of wicked men, stained with footprints of blood. He goes on to talk about Shechem. Now Shechem was a Levitical city, a city full of priest. It was also a city of refuge, meaning that if someone thought he or she might fall victim to a lynch mob before they had a chance to be heard and fairly tried by the councils of their day. They could retreat to Shechem for refuge until trial. But in v9 God said bands of priest were murdering people on the way to Shechem.

When Jesus was telling them to go learn what this means, I truly believe He was wanting them to go read this and get a revelation of what they were doing by deciding for themselves who was and was not worthy of God`s love and grace. When this happens in the church, and it does at times. God is pretty much telling us He sees bloody footprints, and ambushing priest keeping people from their only true refuge, Himself, and His Son the only remedy for their wounds. God help us to see what You see and learn what You want us to learn so we can make the difference we need to make down here till You come.

Post #6

In this week`s Sunday school lesson we read out of the 36 chapter of psalms. In the NIV verses 1,2 David says this. THERE IS AN ORACLE WITHIN MY HEART CONCERNING THE SINFULNESS OF THE WICKED. THERE IS NO FEAR OF GOD BEFORE HIS EYES, FOR IN HIS OWN EYES HE FLATTERS HIMSELF TOO MUCH TO DETECT OR HATE HIS SIN. Hmmm... the wicked don`t hate their own sin. Or you could say it is wicked not to hate your own sin. WOW. We as God's people are supposed to hate the sin and love the sinner and it is easy to hate someone else's sin, but the question is do we hate ours? Jesus said that we are hypocrites if we try to remove the speck from our brother`s eye and ignore the plank in ours, we should remove ours first so we can help others with theirs.

Words of Encouragement

We must hate sin as God does because of its destructive nature, but we should have as much hatred for ours as we do someone else's. Now regarding recent events, I feel I do my best to love everybody, I am not a homophobe, but nor am I soft on sin. I believe what the Bible says is true. Rather I like it or not or you like it or not, it is true, all of it from front to back.

This petition is for my Christian brothers and sisters to be careful that we do not say or do anything to bring the word of God into reproach, that we don't come across as unloving and unconcerned for peoples souls because of a sin you might think especially awful.

We need to be sure that we are not more understanding of other sins and not just this one in question. It is past time for the church to stand up for what is right and not cower to anyone's agenda, but we must also be sure not to misrepresent Jesus and be the cause of anyone to have reason to think we are a hate group. Hearing people say that God destroyed Sodom and Gomorrah because of any certain sin makes me cringe because that is not what the bible says. It says He destroyed it because there was not 10 righteous people there. It says specifically that He would have spared it for 10 righteous people.

When Jesus spoke of Sodom and Gomorrah, He said it would be more tolerable for them on the day of judgement than for the self-righteous, religious leaders of that day. We can stand up for what is right in a loving way, Christ did. We should prepare our hearts for ministry and not just conflict.

God does hate sin, even mine and yours. Let's represent our Savior well in these last days. For they will know you are my disciples because of the love you have for one another. Please stand for what's right, but let's do it right. Jason

Post #7

The topic of falling away and the unpardonable sin has come up lately in conversations. So, I wanted to post a few thoughts on this topic. I don't mean to offend anyone that does not share the same view.

Some of my closest pastor friends do not, but we love one another anyway. They are Godly men and don't use their beliefs for a license to sin, or an excuse to live any way they want. I'm not posting this to raise a debate about anything, but lots of people from all denominations struggle with Hebrews chapter 6:4-6 that says IT IS IMPOSSIBLE FOR THOSE WHO HAVE ONCE BEEN ENLIGHTENED, WHO HAVE TASTED THE HEAVENLY GIFT, WHO HAVE SHARED IN THE HOLY SPIRIT, WHO HAVE TASTED THE GOODNESS OF THE WORD OF GOD AND THE POWERS OF THE COMING AGE, IF THE FALL AWAY, TO BE BROUGHT BACK TO REPENTANCE, BECAUSE TO THEIR LOSS THEY ARE CRUCIFYING THE SON OF GOD ALL OVER

AGAIN AND SUBJECTING HIM TO PUBLIC DISGRACE. This scripture confuses many because most all of us have fallen away at one time or another and were allowed to come back.

What most people don't keep in mind when reading this text is that we are gentiles, and this was wrote to Jews. The writer was warning Jewish Christians that were thinking of departing from faith in Christ to go back to Judaism which means a lot more than simply falling away like we have done. Those Jews were not falling away from God the Father, just Jesus.

Going back to Judaism and the law, they were trying to get to heaven without Christ. In fact, in going back to Judaism they were claiming that Christ was not the Messiah and was not the Son of God that He claimed to be.
So, in doing so they would never be able to find forgiveness because it only comes through Jesus Christ. That is why it was saying they were crucifying Him all over again. When we fell away we were like the prodigal that took what was his and left, not denying who Christ was, but just that we couldn't or didn't want to live for Him at that time, but thank God when we came to our senses He allowed us to come home. We weren't saying Christ was a liar, just not right now.

I believe Hebrews chapter 6 v. 4-6 is the definition of the unpardonable sin. Some believe that the unpardonable sin is pushing the Holy Spirit away and never accepting Christ. But wouldn't that be unforgiven sin and not unforgivable sin? Why would God over and over throughout the scriptures warn us about falling away if it were not possible.

I don't want to make anyone doubt their salvation, but we do need to make our calling and election sure as the Bible tells us to. Again, I don't want to scare anyone or make you doubt your salvation. It has been my observation growing up in church that those scared into going to the altar rarely stayed faithful to God. Please don't let your fear of going to hell be your only motivation to go to heaven.

We should want to go to spend eternity with the One who died for us, paid our sin depth in full and is coming back for those who are ready. He is an awesome God whose love and mercies are new toward us every day. Who wouldn't want to spend eternity with Him? There is an old song that says

I keep falling in love with Him over and over and over and over again He gets sweeter and sweeter as the days go by oh what a love between my Lord and I, I keep falling in love with Him over and over and over and over again. It's not love that we love Him, but that He loves us. Let's go be with Him in Jesus name Amen! Jason

Post #8

Jeremiah 8:10,11 God says FROM THE LEAST TO THE GREATEST, ALL ARE GREEDY FOR GAIN, PROPHET AND PRIEST ALIKE, ALL PRACTICE DECEIT. THEY DRESS THE WOUND OF MY PEOPLE AS THOUGH IT WERE NOT

SERIOUS. Listen, sin is serious... no matter how big or small you might think it is, it's serious. In verse 22 He says. IS THERE NO BALM (salve) IN GILEAD? IS THERE NO PHYSICIAN THERE? WHY THEN IS THERE NO HEALING FOR THE WOUND OF MY PEOPLE? because there is no salve or natural remedy for sin. No bandages or cover ups.

Only Jesus can take away your sin. He is the balm of Gilead, the only remedy for sin is His blood that was shed for you. For your forgiveness, reconciliation, regeneration, and freedom from all that binds. Thank you, Lord for the healing of this crippling, disabling, cancerous, flesh eating, life altering, extremely contagious disease called sin. You must turn to Him if you want your healing.

Post #9

At the end of Jeremiah chapter 7 and beginning of chapter 8 God describes a horrifying site of what it was going to look like around Jerusalem after the Babylonians destroyed everything because they refused to repent. He spoke of multitudes of dead bodies and said they would drag the bones of their dead kings, officials, priest, and people out of their graves to lay on the ground under the sun, moon, and stars.

The things they loved and worshipped, as if to say see if they help you. It's terrible to think that this was probably the last mental picture they had of their homeland before being drug away into slavery. The awesome thought here is that a few years later in Babylon Ezekiel prophesied in chapter 37 about a valley of dry bones. Wow God was giving them hope in Him no matter how they might have viewed the situation. He said, prophesy to those bones. We know how the chapter goes, those bones came together, flesh came and wrapped around them and they stood up an exceedingly Great army. The things of this world cannot help us, but with God all things are possible. We just need to speak the WORD over our lives and believe. Then watch God bring things together.

Post #10

Galatians 5:1 tells us IT WAS FOR FREEDOM THAT DIED TO SET US FREE. Stand firm then, and do not let yourselves be burdened again by a yoke of slavery. In Isaiah chapter 53 a lot of what Christ went through for us to experience our freedom is described. How He took our infirmities and bore our sorrows, pierced for our transgressions, crushed for our iniquities, the punishment that brought us peace was upon Him, by His wounds we are healed, the Lord laid on Him the iniquity of us all. In verse 1 God says WHO HAS BELIEVED OUR MESSAGE AND TO WHOM HAS THE ARM OF THE LORD BEEN REVEALED? I know not everyone believes Gods word and its foolishness to them. But to us that do it's the power of God unto salvation. Sometimes Christians live in defeat, depressed, oppressed, captive do to circumstances of this life.

God wants you to be set free! Believe His word is for you, and get a revelation of His salvation, power, and deliverance we have access to through Jesus the one who sets at Gods right hand praying for you that your faith would not fail, and that you will come out, and be loosed from whatever holds you back, and be the free child of God you need to be for those under you. I pray this happens in your life, in Jesus name Amen. Jason

Post #11

In Luke 2:12 as the angels were announcing the birth of the savior to those shepherds, they told them that THIS WOULD BE A SIGN TO YOU, YOU WILL FIND THE BABY WRAPPED IN SWADDLING CLOTHES LYING IN A MANGER. What they would see would be a sign to them.

To us we might have just seen a baby, but they were temple shepherds watching over and caring for the future sacrifices in the temple. Note that they weren't told where to go, but they hurried off to see this sign. MICAH 4:8 prophecies about the messiah coming to the watch tower of the flock, which was in Bethlehem and the shepherds used the bottom of this tower for birthing stalls for all the ewes that would deliver the temple sacrifices.

They would take these newborn lambs and wrap them in swaddling clothes and lay them in a manger to keep them from being blemished in any way. Ironically enough they used old priestly garments to do this. So, they saw THE future sacrifice for the sins of the whole world laying there in that same manger.

Christ was born exactly where the scriptures said He would be, and if you think about it there is no other place He could have been born. Just something to ponder on this Christmas season, be blessed, and MERRY CHRISTMAS

Post 12

In the end of Luke chapter 7. Luke records a beautiful passage of scripture of Jesus being anointed by a woman of questionable character. He gives a short parable about he who is forgiven much loves much. I had a different thought while studying this last time. If my forgiveness is proportionate to my acknowledgment and confession.

Then I think there is a lot of us in churches everywhere like that Pharisee that need to be forgiven of much. But we can't be forgiven of much because of our lack of confession. In another place in scripture Jesus told the Pharisees that because they think they see their sin remains.

You don't have to come out of a bad background to be able to love much, but you do have to be obedient. I don't think Jesus was telling the Pharisee that he didn't have need of much forgiveness, but the woman in the story was the only one that realized that she truly needed it. No matter what background you come out of we are all obligated to love much. Have a blessed day!

Words of Encouragement

Post #13

In Psalms chapter 11 the writer asks the question. When the foundations are destroyed, what are the righteous to do? Don`t we sometimes feel like things are crumbling down around us. But he gives us the answer in the next verse when he writes. The Lord is in His holy temple, and His throne in heaven. No matter what is going on never forget God is still on the throne and still more than able.

Post #14

I know the bible says that sin separates us from God, and I have and do feel the distance it causes at times in my own life. I am thankful that I serve a God that`s not scared of my sin. The distance we feel is ourselves moving away from Him, not Him moving away from us. God isn't scared of our weaknesses or failures.

He wants nothing more than to empower us to be overcomers. Jesus was never afraid to dine with or embrace sinners to get the chance minister to them. Don`t allow the devil to convince you to stay in your sin or circumstances because you think God is distancing Himself from you, but let God pick you up and establish you as His child. There is nothing about you that scares God.

Words of Encouragement

Post #15

In Jeremiah chapter 38 the prophet Jeremiah gets put in a cistern with no water, just mud and left there to die. Verse 6 says he sank down in the mud. Now thank God he was rescued. And later in the chapter gets to tell the king what God had revealed to him. He told the king that it was him (Zedekiah) that was stuck in the mud because of his friends that he had been listening to and not God.

Jeremiah was receiving revelation from God for someone else in the middle of his persecution. These scriptures really challenged me this week. You see people are more important than our trials. I wonder how much we miss out on because we are to, consumed with our circumstances. Let`s try to be sure that we keep ears to hear, even when we are going through our trials. Be blessed.

Post #16

In Judges chapter 16 we read the account of Samson and Delilah. Most of us know how the story goes. Samson flirts with the enemy and compromises his beliefs and finds himself powerless, bound, blind, out of relationship, captive and grinding at a mill.

We read towards the end of the chapter that after a while his hair begin to grow again. Then one day they brought him into one of their temples to make fun of him. In v28 Samson prayed that the Lord would remember him and strengthen him once more, and God did just that.

The thing I have always missed while reading through these scriptures is that before Samson prayed, he asked to be led over to the pillars that support the temple. You see he put himself in the place for victory. I think that's big part of why we struggle with so many things at times. We don't put ourselves in the place for victory, and believe God for it

Post #17

Jeremiah 17: 1,2 JUDAHS SIN IS ENGRAVED WITH AN IRON TOOL, INSCRIBED WITH A FLINT POINT, ON THE TABLETS OF THEIR HEART'S AND ON THE HORNS OF THEIR ALTARS. EVEN THEIR CHILDREN REMEMBER THEIR ALTARS AND ASHERAH POLES BESIDE THE SPREADING TREE'S AND ON THE HIGH HILLS. When are we going to realize the true victims of our sin? Our sin doesn't just affect us. God help us to live lives pleasing to you so our kid's minds aren't branded with things that might lead them away from you.

Post #18

Isaiah 40:31 THEY THAT WAIT UPON THE LORD SHALL RENEW THEIR STRENGTH, THEY SHALL MOUNT UP ON WINGS AS EAGLES, THEY SHALL RUN, AND NOT BE WEARY, AND THEY SHALL WALK, AND NOT FAINT. I know we think we wait longer than we should have to at sometimes, but this promise was given to those that were told they would be exiled for 70 years. Wow. Kind of puts my problems in perspective. They were told to wait on the Lord, not just for their circumstances to change but to wait on the Lord.

There is a difference. And the strength to walk and run and wings to fly, were so they could take a 800 plus mile trek home, (or back to Him). Where are you running to? What direction are you headed? He may not give us the strength we sometimes pray for just

so we can run away from Him. Oh, but what He won't do for those willing to trust in HIM for that journey home. Lord help me to desire You more than just a change in my circumstances, and help me to move in the direction You have planned for me so I can continue to get closer to You

Post #19

The last few weeks I have been preaching on not being held captive to our past failures, present circumstances, or our preconceived ideas of our future. Last week Brother Terry Green came and delivered a powerful message of how God is the Lifter of our heads and the One that bestows glory upon us, and the Shield around us. Thank you, Brother Terry. Hebrews 3:13 says. ENCOURAGE ONE ANOTHER DAILY, AS LONG AS IT IS CALLED TODAY, SO THAT NONE OF YOU WILL BE HARDENED BY SINS DECEITFULNESS. Be encouraged today in the fact that God cannot love you any more or less than He already does. Encourage someone today. We can't do it yesterday, and tomorrow may not afford the same opportunity. Be blessed, stay warm and safe.

Post #20

I hope everyone has a blessed Resurrection Sunday tomorrow. I have been preaching through the book of Isaiah for some time now. Tomorrow I Will be going back to chapter 25 and preaching on some awesome prophecies about what Christ did for us

on Calvary almost 800 years later. Chapter 25 is a song of praise to the Lord, it starts out praising Him for His perfect faithfulness, and marvelous things done, things planned long ago.

Deliverance from enemies. And then in verses 6-9 He says ON THIS MOUNTAIN THE LORD ALMIGHTY WILL PREPARE A FEAST OF RICH FOOD FOR ALL PEOPLES, A BANQUET OF AGED WINE -THE BEST MEATS AND THE FINEST OF WINES. ON THIS MOUNTAIN HE WILL DESTROY THE SHROUD THAT ENFOLDS ALL PEOPLES, THAT SHEET THAT COVERS ALL NATIONS. HE WILL SWALLOW UP DEATH FOREVER. THE SOVEREIGN LORD WILL WIPE AWAY THE TEARS FROM ALL FACES; HE WILL REMOVE THE DISGRACE OF HIS PEOPLE FROM ALL THE EARTH. THE LORD HAS SPOKEN. IN THAT DAY THEY WILL SAY, SURELY THIS IS OUR GOD; WE TRUSTED IN HIM AND HE SAVED US. THIS IS THE LORD, WE TRUSTED IN HIM, LET US REJOICE AND BE GLAD IN HIS SALVATION. This is what Christ died for, to do this for us almost 2000 years ago.

On that very mountain He destroyed that shroud of mourning and heaviness and swallowed up death forever and removed our disgrace. Oh people let us rejoice in His salvation. WHERE O DEATH, IS YOUR VICTORY? WHERE O DEATH, IS YOUR STING. THE STING OF DEATH IS SIN, THE POWER OF SIN IS THE LAW. BUT THANKS BE TO GOD! HE GIVES US VICTORY THROUGH OUR LORD JESUS CHRIST. (1 COR.

15:55,56) Lets not just praise Him tomorrow for these MARVELOUS THINGS PLANNED LONG AGO but Lets, praise Him forever for them!! Thank you, Christ for taking our place on that cross, help us to live our lives in a manner that brings You glory. in Jesus name amen. Jason.

Post #21

In 1 Chronicles 22:1,2 King David gave orders for where the House of the Lord should be built, and appointed stonecutters to prepare dressed stone for the building of the House of God. The thing I had never noticed or really even thought about was who was ordered to do it? I guess I just always thought that the Jews done everything. But v2 says he ordered the aliens or foreigners living in Israel to be appointed stonecutters.

This struck me funny for a bit with all the regulations they had on who could even enter the temple. But the Jews were mainly farmers, shepherd's, fishermen. Not master builders, but thankfully there were some in the land.

Words of Encouragement

I just thought it ironic that most of these more than likely learned their trade building temples to false gods and carving idols, but now that they had more than likely converted to Judaism because they were living in the land. God was going to use them to build His temple. I'm sure glad we serve a God that uses ex idol makers/worshipers/ gentiles to not only build His temple but BE the temple of God. Living stones to be built into a spiritual house, a holy

priesthood that we may declare the praises of Him who called us out of darkness into His marvelous light.

When I first read it, I thought, now that's weird, but then the more I thought about it, I thought well that's just like God to do that, and He doesn't make mistakes. Blessings

Post #22

In Isaiah 7:14 king Ahaz was told that THE LORD HIMSELF WOULD GIVE YOU A SIGN, THE VIRGIN WILL BE WITH CHILD AND GIVE BIRTH TO A SON AND WE WILL CALL HIM IMMANUEL. This prophecy means more than just God with us. In context the sign was given to Ahaz because he was believing the lie of the enemy, that they were going to come destroy them and there was nothing he could do about it and the people were in fear.

God promised the sign to show that He was not only with them but would destroy their enemies, and bring real salvation, peace, and the safety they desired and was looking for in other things rather than God, and He did. Then 700 some years later God fulfills this scripture again in the birth of Christ, to not only be with us but destroy death, hell, and the grave. To bring salvation, peace, joy, restoration, power over sin, victory over our enemies. He's your sign of salvation and victory if you will just believe, Merry Christmas everyone

Post #23

I think it's neat to sometimes see the human side of the superheroes of our faith, like Elijah in 1 Kings chapter 18 and 19 Elijah meets up with Israel's wicked king Ahab and 450 prophets of Baal for a showdown on mount Carmel. Ahab had been trying to find and kill Elijah for the last few years. Elijah calls fire down from heaven then kills 450 prophets of Baal and prays and it rains, supernaturally out runs a chariot, all in one day. WOW what a day.

Then in the same day gets word that the queen wants to kill him, and he takes off running scared all the way to mount Sinai. That's over 350 miles south from Carmel. Wow again. The funny thing is God sent an angel to feed him and strengthen him for the journey. When he got there, God asked him what he was doing there because God didn't tell him to go there, but God did minister to him on the way. You see just because God is being good to us doesn't always mean we are heading in the right direction. That's just how good God is.

After him and God got some things worked out God told him to go back the way he came. God sent him 450 miles north from where he ran to. Wow again. It makes me wonder how far out of the way we go when we don`t live by faith and allow fear and unbelief to creep in our lives at times. The bible says God doesn't give us a spirit of fear, but power, love and a sound mind. He is going out before you, in whatever it is your facing. Jason

Post #24

In Deuteronomy chapter 4 Moses is warning the children of Israel not to fall into idolatry after they go into the promise land, and not to forget their covenant with God. Moses told them that if this happened that they would be scattered among the nations with few survivors, exiled and there they would worship these gods of wood and stone. But verse 29 I think is exceptionally awesome, it says. V 29. But if from there you seek the Lord your God, you will find Him if you look for Him with all your heart and all your soul. Wow, no matter how far away we are driven by sin if we search for Him, He will be found. I know as Gods people we cannot be soft on sin, and we must call it how it is. But let`s not forget to be big on GRACE because that`s how He is. (But if from there) that`s right where you are. Turn to Him, and you will find Him, why? because He is there with you. I hope you do or have. Jason

Post #25

Part of Amos 3:12 says. AS A SHEPHERD SAVES FROM THE LIONS MOUTH ONLY TWO LEG BONES OR A PIECE OF AN EAR, SO WILL THE ISRAELITES BE SAVED, I'm sure glad the Lord is willing to save the pieces of our lives when we have been torn apart by sin, and make us new again. With just a piece of an ear... Your, never too far gone for God. Be encouraged tonight in Jesus name amen.

Post #26

In Isaiah chapter 26 Isaiah records a song of praise that most of us would recognize parts of. I recently found these first few verses to be very encouraging. It says WE HAVE A STRONG CITY; GOD MAKES SALVATION ITS WALLS AND RAMPARTS. OPEN THE GATES THAT THE RIGHTEOUS NATION MAY ENTER, THE NATION THAT KEEPS FAITH. YOU WILL KEEP IN PERFECT PEACE HIM WHOSE MIND IS STEADFAST, BECAUSE HE TRUSTS IN YOU. TRUST IN THE LORD FOREVER, FOR THE LORD, THE LORD, IS THE ROCK ETERNAL. This is an awesome reminder that we belong to God, and that as people of faith we do have a STRONG CITY and that God is our protector He is our walls, our refuge.

This passage says OPEN THE GATES that the righteous that keep the faith may enter. As if to say, if you want to live in Gods city you must enter by faith. We receive our salvation the same way, through faith. I want Gods salvation to be my walls, not my ability, accomplishments, job, 401k, doctors, etc.... Its God that will keep us in HIS PERFECT PEACE whose mind is steadfast on Him. We could all do a better job trusting in Him and would benefit from it. Verse 2 says the gate is open, I'm going in, are you coming with me? Jason.

Post #27

Have you ever experienced mental or spiritual fatigue or felt burned out? I sure have. A couple of years ago I was experiencing it worse than ever before. And one day I was reading in Mark Ch. 6 and the Lord showed me something that changed my life. Of course, chapter 6 is filled with all sorts of awesome sermon material, but because of my state of mind I noticed something new. The disciples were back from being sent out 2 by 2 and trying to tell Jesus about everything, and they couldn't because of the crowds. They couldn't even eat lunch.

So, they tried to go to a quiet place, just them and Jesus, boy that sure seemed nice to me, I felt like I needed a long vacation. So, they sailed across the sea of Galilee only to be met by 5000 men not counting women and kids. I felt bad for the disciples, I guess there's no rest for the weary, or that's how we feel sometimes. After feeding the 5000 Jesus sends them back across the sea without Him, and well we all know they were sent headlong into the storm of their life.

Now I really felt bad for them, because of what I was going through I almost felt like I was right there with them. I know Jesus was about to do something about the storm, but they still don't have rest. As soon as the storm is over and they get to the other side, they are met by crowds again, right out of the boat. I was like man God when are they going to find that quiet place and rest. Then He said to me *peace and rest don't come from ceasing to labor, they come from Me*. That was a huge revelation to me that changed everything.

We need to receive His rest, peace, strength, calm from Him in the middle of our chaos because the chaos more than likely isn't going to change. But we sure can. God do the work in us that needs

to be done, so we can continue to do what needs to be done. Your peace and joy come from Him, and they are a choice. Chose them today. Jason

Post #28

Isaiah 57:16-19 says I WILL NOT ACCUSE FOREVER, NOR WILL I ALWAYS BE ANGRY, FOR THEN THE SPIRIT OF MAN WILL GROW FAINT BEFORE ME, THE BREATH OF MAN THAT I HAVE CREATED. I WAS ENRAGED BY HIS SINFUL GREED, I PUNISHED HIM, AND HID MY FACE IN ANGER, YET HE KEPT ON IN HIS WILLFUL WAYS. I HAVE SEEN HIS WAYS, BUT I WILL HEAL HIM. I WILL GUIDE HIM AND RESTORE COMFORT TO HIM, CREATING PRAISE ON THE LIPS OF THE MOURNERS IN ISRAEL. PEACE, PEACE, TO THOSE FAR AND NEAR, SAYS THE LORD. I WILL HEAL THEM. Wow to think that God knows everything about us, how willingly sinful we can be. But chooses to love and minister to us.

To forgive, heal, guide, comfort, restore, and give peace to those who would accept it is awesome and convicting, life changing, it's GOD!!! He is beyond good to us. V 19 said CREATING PRAISE ON THE LIPS OF THE MOURNERS IN ISRAEL. Israel's physical situation hadn't changed yet. But God was promising to change their spiritual, mental state first.

God wants to exchange all your sorrows, and fears for peace, joy, and gladness. V21 says THERE IS NO PEACE FOR THE

WICKED. That's because most of the things like peace, and joy are not accomplishments. They are gifts from God that we need to choose to walk in. It's not love that we love Him, its love that He loves us. Jason

Post #29

In Isaiah chapter 59 we see Isaiah describe Israel's sinful state, and confession, then redemption. The same order in which man receives salvation today. Acknowledge, and confess your sin, believe Jesus is the Son of God, and by faith except the redemptive work He went through on the cross for you. In verse 16 it says. HE SAW THAT THERE WAS NO ONE, HE WAS APPALLED THAT THERE WAS NO ONE TO INTERVENE, SO HIS OWN ARM WORKED SALVATION FOR HIM, AND HIS OWN RIGHTEOUSNESS SUSTAINED HIM. 17 HE PUT ON RIGHTEOUSNESS AS HIS BREASTPLATE, AND THE HELMET OF SALVATION ON HIS HEAD, HE PUT ON

GARMENTS OF VENGEANCE, AND WRAPPED HIMSELF IN ZEAL AS A CLOAK. Garments of vengeance were blood splattered garments.

God was promising to do this to free them from slavery and there was no one else that could do it. Christ did this for us, and there was no one else that could. He won us the victory and freedom we needed as He wrapped Himself in our stripes, our bruises, our crown

of thorns, and our cross. He will come in vengeance again. I hope you are on the right side. Jason

Acknowledgements

I would like to thank everyone that helped and took part in making this book happen. For helping me fulfill what God had asked me to do. There are too many to name, but you know who you are, thank you from the bottom of my heart. I pray God blesses you all in everything you endeavor to do for Him. This has been quite the journey and the farthest out of my comfort zone I've been in a long time. Thank you to all my alpha readers that read draft after draft and gave good helpful and encouraging feedback, it really helped. Thank you to all who helped work on the cover art. I know it was hard for you guys to capture what I have had stuck in my head for several years now, but every one of you got me closer to my cover.

Thank you, God Bless you.

Sincerely,

Jason Moppin

www.ingramcontent.com/pod-product-compliance
Lightning Source LLC
Chambersburg PA
CBHW071351080526
44587CB00017B/3057